DISTRIBUTION PLANNING AND CONTROL

Distribution planning and control

A corporate approach

MARTIN CHRISTOPHER
DAVID WALTERS
with
JOHN GATTORNA

A Gower Press Special Study

HF
5415.7
C 47

Published by
Gower Press, Teakfield Limited,
Westmead, Farnborough, Hants., England

ISBN 0 566 02013 0

Photoset by Amos Typesetters, Hockley, Essex
Printed in Great Britain by Biddles Ltd of Guildford, Surrey

92616

Contents

Table

Figures

Preface

The last ten years or so have seen a growing recognition of the importance of the distribution function in all sections of industry. At the same time, there has been a marked increase in the number of books, articles, short courses, conferences and seminars devoted to the subject. In the United States the National Council for Physical Distribution Management, and in the United Kingdom the Centre for Physical Distribution Management have acted as catalysts in this upsurge of interest.

Our own book examines in detail two crucial aspects of the distribution function: its planning and its control. These twin tasks are too often neglected. In many firms distribution is viewed as a mechanical task and managerial effort is devoted solely to the reduction of costs. But cost minimisation and profit maximisation rarely coincide. In this book we have tried to show that, by a systematic and rigorous review of possible objectives and an evaluation of the alternative means of achieving those objectives, the company can develop a distribution system that is a positive contributor to profit.

Our aim in writing this book was to present these ideas to the widest possible audience, to distribution and marketing practitioners in both line management and planning functions as well as to that growing body of students who are involved in courses and study programmes in distribution management.

The structure of the book is therefore based upon the need to be practical as well as instructive. It is designed to take the reader in a sequential way through the various tasks of the distribution planning and control activity, from the need to recognise the corporate context of distribution objectives through to a final 'checklist' for performing a distribution audit.

We have taken the established concepts and techniques of planning and control and applied them to the distribution activity. In so doing, we have had to extend considerably current notions of what the distribution planning task should involve. We make no apology for this as we believe that present practice is, for the majority of companies, inadequate. Thus many of the ideas in this book may appear controversial, but we do believe that their careful application will lead to a substantially improved distribution performance.

Martin Christopher
David Walters
John Gattorna

1 Approaching the planning and control problem

The total distribution concept

In recent years there has been a growing recognition of the importance of physical distribution and related activities as a key determinant of corporate performance. Attention has perhaps tended to focus too heavily upon the potential for cost reduction within the distribution activity rather than upon the wider issue of devising integrated distribution policies which can impact both upon costs and revenue.

Central to an understanding of the possibilities that an integrated approach to distribution can provide is the concept of the corporate system. Such a company-wide orientation requires a radically new approach, both to policy determination and to organisational structures. It requires a recognition at a high level within the company that the provision of distribution service and the level at which it is sustained is a strategic and tactical issue of the greatest importance.

In a relatively short space of time Physical Distribution Management (PDM) has become a matter of great managerial concern. PDM in its corporate context refers to all those activities and decisions concerned with the flow of materials and related information through the company system. It thus extends its concern to embrace movements of raw materials, part assemblies and so on into the system, movements within the system, and finally movements of finished goods through the marketing channel to the customer. Its essence would therefore appear to be a concern with flows, flows both of physical entities and of the information related to them. Associated with these physical flows are the activities necessary to their efficient movement: inventory holding, warehousing, transportation, unitisation and handling. Therefore PDM, from this viewpoint, encompasses a wide range of interacting and inter-related elements the co-ordination of which requires new tools and approaches.

A further reason for the growing importance attached to the PDM concept is the awareness of the magnitude of the costs involved in its constituent activities. Various estimates have been made as to the percentage of total corporate costs accounted for by these activities in different industries. Whilst these estimates differ depending upon the

1

nature of the business involved, it seems that PDM costs can account for 20 per cent or more of all costs within a company. It is not difficult to see how such costs can arise when it is realised that total physical distribution costs comprise inventory holding costs, warehouse costs, transportation and handling costs and order processing costs.

Typically, managerial attempts to handle the problems of growing physical distribution costs have been of a piecemeal nature. That is, the individual activity centres have been examined for possible improvements but without regard for the effects that any changes in a single activity might have on other activities. For example, cutting costs on transportation might lead to higher costs elsewhere in the system, for instance inventory holding might grow. It is because of the dangers of such sub-optimisation that PDM, with its emphasis on trade-off analysis and total cost analysis, has come to provide the framework and the tools for a global, systems approach to the problems of managing a complex network of flows which comprise the typical company.

Wedded to the possibility of cost reductions through more efficient management is the prospect of revenue improvement through the provision of a more efficient distribution capability. This means in effect that a co-ordinated approach to distribution can result in higher levels of customer service that may impact upon performance in the market place. Indeed there can be circumstances where higher distribution costs can be justified because of the increase in marketing effectiveness. There has perhaps been rather too much emphasis on cost cutting in distribution and too little regard for the total cost benefit of system performance. There are two sides to the profit coin and long term profit enhancement can only be achieved by considering the implications for both cost and revenue of specific logistics strategies.

The planning activity

The company and its customers are separated by space and time. The spatial separation is geographic and can be overcome by an efficient transport network, but the temporal separation results from the more fundamental lag between the time of production and the time of consumption. The two considerations of space and time are obviously linked and distribution strategies must recognise the effects of a decision taken affecting the one upon the performance of the other.

It will be suggested later in this book that a systems approach to logistics thinking and planning can be beneficial in overcoming the problems of managing complex flow networks. However, the systems approach has a far greater power than simply enabling the planner to gain a better understanding of the logistics activity. Because of its emphasis on inputs and outputs it forces the planner to consider the connections between the two. These connections and the way they function are the crucial determinants of system performance. The second law of thermo-dynamics tells us that the entropy, i.e. disorder, of systems tends naturally to increase. This is as true of a management system as it is of a physical system. This tendency to disorder can only be halted by closing the loop between inputs and outputs, by ensuring that through a 'feedback' mechanism the system is producing the output that the market place requires and that we have the correct balance of inputs to achieve those outputs. This in essence is the purpose of the planning activity within the company.

In any business activity planning and control are of primary importance. A case can be made for a bold statement: without an effective planning and control system the business cannot function effectively – or for long!

What is a planning and control system? The fundamentals are described in a simple form in Figure 1.1.

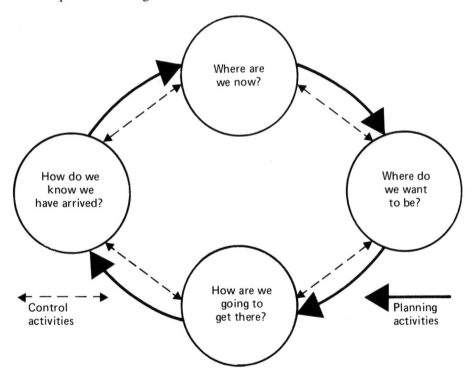

Figure 1.1   The planning and control cycle

A few words of explanation at this stage will serve to set the scene. Any business planner must start with a thorough knowledge of the current situation stands. He must also be aware of the reasons why the firm is in this particular situation. Furthermore, the planner must also have a detailed knowledge of the company's operating environment.

The operating environment of the firm can be defined as the framework of constraints and opportunities within which the firm operates and as such an external environment and an internal environment can be identified. The external environment comprises a number of features such as:

(a) competitive structure;
(b) marketing channels utilised;
(c) market dynamics;
(d) legal and institutional framework, etc.

The internal environment on the other hand comprises those aspects of the corporate system that determine the way we currently operate. For example, such factors as:

(a) sales volumes;
(b) product mix and characteristics;
(c) systems costs;
(d) fixed facilities such as plant and depots;
(e) resource availability, i.e. finance, management, etc.

Clearly, the distribution planner must identify the current nature of these environments as a first requirement in the planning process. This is, of course, an auditing activity and in planning terms is the *Position Audit* to which we will return.

Where do we want to be? Most companies have a vague idea of what they would like the future to hold for them. Some attempt to be positive and appraise their current situation with a view to developing a plan for the future. However, very few devote a great deal of time to this task and, of those that do, few make their intentions explicit. Underlying this basic activity is the process of establishing two crucial factors. Firstly, the company is asking itself: 'What is our business (or businesses)?' Secondly, having resolved that, the company goes on to ask: 'What should our objectives be?'

Much has been written in these two areas and it is not the purpose of this book to add to the vast literature that has already accumulated. However, it is our intention to extract appropriate concepts and develop them in the context of distribution planning and control.

4

Possibly one of the most useful contributions to the planning and control problem is that made by Tilles [1] who suggests that: 'Few things determine the future of the company as directly as the way it spends its money'. Tilles, in discussing the problems surrounding investment decisions, points to what he describes as the 'organisational fallacy'. This he sees as the conflicting logic where planning takes place at different levels. He suggests that while, for example, the purpose of an investment programme is to enhance the performance of the total corporate entity, the logic for creating divisions, departments or groups is a different logic from that underlying the allocation of funds.

Planning involves allocating resources, which presumably for most companies are scarce. It would therefore appear that the most rational method would be one which allocates resources on such a basis as to maximise 'total' company performance.

The planning system must be capable of identifying and considering all those alternatives which provide a basis for the strategic allocation of capital resources.

What then are the alternatives? Tilles (op. cit.) suggested four:

1 *Product portfolio:* in which the return from a package of products is managed and evaluated in terms of return (and risk) from a specific investment.
2 *Geographic area:* in which the firm's business is managed and funded strictly in terms of territorial areas.
3 *Distinctive competence:* whereby specific expertise is identified and reinforced by continued investment.
4 *The missions concept:* whereby the fundamental purpose(s) that the organisation is trying to achieve is identified and used as the basis for planning.

While each of these alternatives offers advantages, it is the missions concept that has particular attraction in the context of distribution planning and control.

The idea of the 'mission' is simple: it is an attempt to look at the overall activities of the firms and to identify the 'fundamental purposes that organisation is trying to achieve' (Tilles op. cit.). It is based upon the notion that every company should ask itself the question: 'What businesses are we in?' and that the answer should be described more in terms of the basic market needs that it is attempting to satisfy rather than in terms of the products that it produces. As such the concept of the mission is very much 'output-oriented' rather than 'input-oriented'. At the same time the definition of missions must take account of the company's existing technology and manufacturing base and its franchise with the market place.

Having arrived at a suitable definition of the company's business we must delineate goals or objectives: this is the other aspect of the 'Where do we want to be?' decision. Within a business organisation we find that there is a need for both economic and non-economic objectives.

Economic objectives relate the activities of the firm to such things as profitability, sales turnover, market share, sales per territory, etc. In other words they are quantitative measures of aspects of performance. Non-economic objectives relate to such aspects of business operations as staff development, environmental considerations and consumer choice.

There is evidence to suggest that most firms are guided in their decision making behaviour by considerations other than the meeting of economic objectives. Within the organisation there will be a complex pattern of individual and group goals, some congruent, some in conflict. Because of the informal nature of these goals—informal in the sense that they may never be precisely stated—the task of the planner in determining the objectives of the firm is made more difficult. Yet if these human,

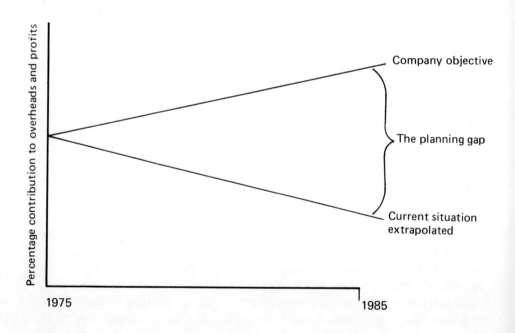

Figure 1.2   The initial planning gap

qualitative goals are not somehow encompassed within the plan then the plan will have a greatly reduced chance of working.

Given that we know where we want to go, how do we get where we want to be? Strategy relates the planning decisions that are required to reach the composite objectives from the current position (as established by the position audit).

The requirement for strategy can be seen quite simply in terms of the so-called 'planning gap'. The planning gap is simply the difference between where we want to be at the end of our planning horizon and where we will materially be if we simply continue the way we are.

Figure 1.2 takes a hypothetical examination of the planning gap that is shown as developing over a ten year planning horizon. The role of strategy is to present the means of filling that gap.

Ansoff [2] has provided a useful classification of the way in which strategy may be developed and Figure 1.3 examines his approach. He suggests that basically there are two dimensions along which the company may develop. The first is a Market dimension, the second a Product dimension. We could, for instance, stay with our existing products in our

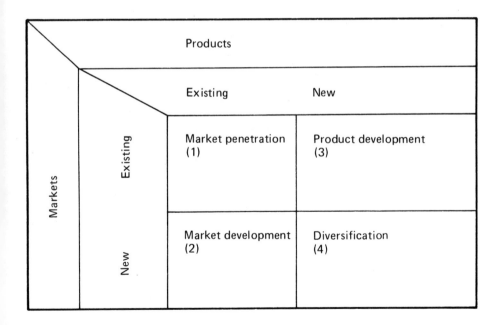

Figure 1.3 Ansoff's product/market mission matrix

existing markets but try to sell more of those products – this is the strategy of 'market penetration'. Such a strategy might involve increased advertising expenditure, improved distribution coverage, reduced prices and so on. This strategy corresponds to Quadrant 1 in Figure 1.3.

Other strategies that are available are those of 'market development' (Quadrant 2) 'product development' (Quadrant 3) and 'diversification' (Quadrant 4). Each of these strategies involves moving from an existing area into new territories and whilst market development and product development each maintain at least a contact with an existing expertise the diversification strategy involves the highest potential risk, having no linkage with existing expertise.

In each of these strategic options there will be considerable implications for distribution planning and any development of corporate strategy must give the fullest consideration to the role of distribution.

From the development of strategies the next stage is the preparation of programmes and plans on a functional basis. In other words programmes and plans must be developed for the marketing function, the operations function, the distribution function and so on. These programmes and plans are not developed independently of each other, but through the mechanism of the overall corporate plan these are closely integrated and related.

The last activity in Figure 1.1 was: 'How do we know we have arrived?' This is crucial to the planning and control system. There are two aspects: the first is knowing what to measure, the second is knowing how often to measure it. Possibly these suggest a third: knowing what action to take if performance varies from desired standards. This is our *Performance Audit.*

Planning and controlling the physical distribution activity: some current thoughts

At this juncture we will pause and examine just a few of the distribution planning and control procedures that have been proposed in the literature during recent years.

Early contributions have tended to concentrate on the cost aspects of budgetary control. Wilson [3] outlines a control system which is based upon an annual operating plan. He suggests that the annual operating plan should comprise of operating budget, capital budget, financial budget and personnel budget.

The operating budget usually details costs by functional activity. For distribution these are storage, handling, trunking operations, delivery, workshops and maintenance. The capital budget is based upon a review of physical resources which will be required during the year of the operating plan and in future periods. Expenditure required for expansion should be shown separately from that required for replacement programmes. The financial budget links the operating and capital expenditure budgets so as to incorporate financial transactions, such as depreciation, taxation, capital allowances, investment grants, etc., together with changes in levels of current assets and liabilities. The personnel budget incorporates a statement in terms of both numbers and cost of the various grades of personnel which are required.

Budget preparation involves management at all levels. The flow of information needs to be subject both to quality control and schedule controls – accurate and timely information is crucial. Costs are derived from use of resources and the levels of resources will be determined from the sales forecast in the marketing budget. Changes in cost levels should be determined for those resources likely to increase or decrease during the budgetary period.

The completed budget provides information to top management for their review of the ensuing year's total plan, and in detail by cost centres to each departmental/regional manager for the cost of the activities under his control. Wilson suggests that the budget becomes the focal point by which control can be maintained and the means by which authority can be allocated and delegated.

Budgets are not easily (or cheaply) prepared, hence all will be wasted unless they become the tools for monitoring the actual results of operations. By involving all levels of management in preparing the budgets their acceptance of resource levels and costs should be assured. Obviously there will be problems and Wilson suggests (with some foresight) that inflation should be dealt with by building flexibility into the budget system. In addition, variations in the level of activity will result in lower or higher costs and these costs should be segregated from those that remain static or fixed. This enables the efficient utilisation of fixed assets to be monitored and highlighted.

Communications are vital. Information should be supplied to managers showing performance of those activities within their responsibility. If possible the revenues generated by their activities should also be credited to them.

Wilson suggests a series of key ratios as essential indicators of changes in the levels of activity, unitisation, costs and revenues. However, ratios have both numerator and denominator and significant changes must be investigated from both points of view. Stock turn ratios for example can be improved either by increasing sales or by decreasing inventory levels. The implications of each are very different.

Standard costs can prove useful as yardsticks against which actual results can be compared. They may be time taken for an operation, materials usage, labour required or process costs. Standard costing is based upon the principle that actual expense can be compared with the cost based upon previously calculated standards. Standards are based upon performances which are at high levels of efficiency and which are attainable. Wilson makes a very pertinent point concerning the high, fixed cost content of distribution systems as much of the overtime payment to labour is incorporated into basic rates. As the problem of control concerns fixed expenditure items, administration costs may become excessive thereby resulting in the use of standards for controlling those items for which expense varies in a direct linear relationship with the activity. Such systems rely upon a strict budgetary control of the level of fixed resources, while using standard costs as the control for variable expenses, and maintaining stringent controls over the efficiencies and utilisation of both personnel and equipment.

At a detailed day to day level of operation this system is ideal. It enables close control to be maintained and highlights deficiencies promptly. However, it is of limited use in the longer term planning of distribution systems. Nevertheless, the cost data bank which is inevitably built up through such budgetary control systems can provide a valuable input to the eventual development of an on-going auditing system.

Bowersox et al [4] approach the problem from a broader context. They suggest:

> The most important part of the total design process is the distribution audit. The audit is aimed at the development of information to be used in the design study. As such, all that follows centers around the search process of data collection. Focal points in a comprehensive audit are divided as follows: (1) product profile, (2) market profile, (3) competitive profile, (4) existing facility profile, (5) measurement standards and cost profile. Each profile contains information for design and manipulation of the system model . . . The typical audit will require considerable research effort to collect the necessary data.

This is a more useful approach. It combines the cost data generated in the previous approach with information on a number of extremely relevant topics. It is worthwhile to consider each of these topics briefly:

Product profile. The product profile aims at delineating the firm's product assortment which directly relate to the physical distribution process such as:

1 Current packaging (sizes and protective performance requirements).
2 Special handling (size and shelf-life requirements).
3 Annual volume (flow capacity in PD system design and flow variations).
4 Profitability (product group interdependence and assortment profitability).
5 Marketing channel congruity.

Market profile. The market profile quantifies current and potential customer demands for individual products. It seeks answers to such questions as: Who are our current customers? How much do they buy of each product? What is a reasonable estimate of future requirements? What special services do they require? Where are they located from a physical distribution viewpoint? This is basic information for system design. Emphasis should be placed upon service as this can be a major source of new business and a major factor in keeping existing business.

Competitive profile. Two sources of information are of interest – competitors' customers who clearly are target prospects and the quality of service regularly offered by competitive firms. Specifically, service levels, delivery times and reliability are of interest. The critical issue is not only the opportunity such lack of competitive performance offers but also the reduction of the danger of attempting to design a system to eliminate a non-existent competitive advantage.

Existing facility profile. This profile includes capacity, operating cost level, capabilities, expansion possibilities and 'life expectancy'. Life expectancy is important for two reasons – as a financial expression of fixed capital committed in terms of depreciation schedules (and hence cash flow) and from the point of view of the impact of potential real cost changes on future system economics.

Measurement standards and cost profile. Two aspects arise. Firstly, cost centres must be identified and established; secondly, trade off potentials must be identified (the application of a systems approach whereby costs of one activity may consciously be increased in order to lower the overall total costs of operations or possibly to increase profitability). In addition it is essential to develop cross-departmental cost measures as well as an approximation of the reaction of costs to different levels of throughput.

Summary

This initial chapter has attempted to introduce the reader to the planning and control of business operations. A general picture was established to make the point that business planning (and control) must be an integrated activity in order that individual functional plans will evolve.

Against this general background specific physical distribution system auditing systems have been discussed. In doing this we have attempted to establish the fact that while each is effective it could be more so if developed as part of the corporate planning activity. Furthermore, it is essential that as a plan is developed so too must the audit procedure be. This latter point will be developed at much greater length in subsequent chapters.

Chapter 2 develops the corporate/marketing planning topic and demonstrates the need for PDM to be considered against corporate objectives and strategies.

Notes

[1] S. Tilles, 'Strategies for Allocating Funds', *Harvard Business Review*, January/February 1966.
[2] I. Ansoff, *Corporate Strategy*, McGraw Hill, 1965.
[3] F. W. Wilson, 'Distribution Budgeting and Control Systems', in F. Wentworth (ed) *Physical Distribution Management*, Gower Press, 1970.
[4] D. Bowersox, E. Smykay and B. LaLonde, *Physical Distribution Management*, Macmillan, London 1968.

2 Relating corporate planning to PDM

Introduction

In the previous chapter a number of basic issues were established which are central to the major theme of this book: the planning and control of a company's physical distribution system. We first reviewed the total distribution concept and made the point that to be successfully implemented it must be seen in the context of the complete corporate system. The second point concerned the planning process itself which, it was argued, must include a control function if the plan was to serve any useful purpose. Finally, we reviewed a number of planning/audit approaches: the conclusion being that the closer the distribution planning and auditing activity is to the corporate plan, the more effective it would appear to become. The purpose of this chapter is to examine this last part in more detail. First, we must establish what we mean by corporate planning and how corporate planning and physical distribution interact. It will be seen that there are numerous implications for physical distribution in corporate decisions and these are best understood by first examining the corporate planning activity itself.

Corporate planning and its implications for PDM

Figure 2.1 shows the total corporate planning activity and illustrates the high degree of interdependence between all functional areas at the planning level. Let us look at the key activities shown in this figure. Consider first the Corporate Position Audit. Earlier we suggested that its purpose was to establish the current position of the organisation. Usually this comprises three activities: a review of past performance, an internal audit to examine the company's strengths and weaknesses and an external audit aimed at examining the opportunities and threats facing the company.

The review of past performance is primarily a marketing review of the performance of product and product groups within their markets. This usually involves a review of respective product life cycle positions and

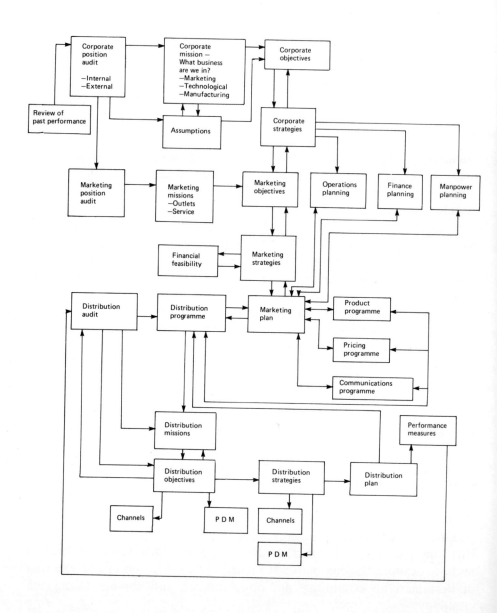

Figure 2.1 Total corporate planning activities

individual product cash generation and requirements. Often included in the review is the performance of the company's products within the channels of distribution and outlets used to reach the consumer.

The second stage of the position audit is the detailed examination of Strengths, Weaknesses, Opportunities and Threats (often termed SWOT analysis for short).

A strength is a competence which, if not unique to the company, puts it in a position of advantage relevant to its competitors. Such a strength might be a dominant market share for a particular product. This could provide a number of advantages. For example, the company could possibly dictate pricing policy or maybe, because of very strong brand loyalty, effectively restrict entry into a market. Furthermore, if the company has the dominant share of a market it can seek to exploit its 'monopoly power' in the area of distribution service, operating at those inventory service levels and order cycle lengths, etc., which are most suitable for the company.

The reverse of this situation, a low market share, can be an example of a corporate weakness. A low market share usually implies that the company must be a price follower rather than a price leader. It will have little or no power to prevent new companies from entering the market and, from the point of view of distribution service, it must offer as competitive a level of service as is compatible with costs. Thus a weakness is a constraint, or a limiting factor upon the firm.

Strengths (and weaknesses) are not necessarily just product or market oriented. They can involve a number of aspects:

1 Corporate image.
2 Availability of finance at 'reasonable rates'.
3 Contribution factors.
4 Unit costs.
5 Integration (backward into sources of supply/forward into retail outlets).
6 Managerial expertise.
7 Labour availability.
8 Unbalanced profit/product mix.
9 Unbalanced product portfolio.
10 R and D programmes.
11 Liquidity and cash flow situations.

It should perhaps be emphasised that both strengths and weaknesses are situations that appear at a moment in time and as such should not be considered as permanent features. As Peter Drucker once pointed out: all leadership positions are transitory.

All companies operate within a much larger environment than just their own immediate sphere. They must relate their activities to this larger environment. Specifically they must identify those opportunities and/or threats that are posed by it. Usually this part of the corporate position audit comprises a systematic review of the social, economic, regulatory, competitive and technological aspects of the overall environment. Again some examples may prove useful.

Social

Example: The introduction of legislation regarding non-returnable bottles
The State of Oregon in the USA introduced a Bill in 1972 which stipulated that all beverages sold in that State must be sold in a returnable container which had to have a minimum refundable deposit. Such legislation obviously had profound effects upon the distribution systems of the beverage manufacturers and distributors. The legislation was originally seen by many as a threat in the sense of being an imposition of additional costs. The outcome has been, however, that a whole new distribution and marketing environment has been created which represents as many opportunities as threats. For example, when the distributor has made the once and for all adjustment to his system to handle returns, he gains the benefits of re-using a container up to twenty times.

Examples of this kind of 'social' legislation are becoming increasingly common and emphasise the need for a careful monitor of the external environment to be maintained.

Economic

Example: The quadrupling of oil prices
Again dependent upon the situation this could also be viewed as either an opportunity or a threat. A company offering consolidated distribution as a service will probably view this as an opportunity for, although their operating costs will increase, those of all other operators will also rise and some will opt to buy their distribution service from a consolidation company which is able to achieve the economies of scale that the smaller companies cannot.

Regulatory

Example: Government controls on profit margins
For food retailers this was clearly a threat to their continued profitability. However, opportunities can be found even here. Margin controls suggest

16

the need to review all cost centres for economies. This immediately becomes an opportunity for consultants and systems companies as well as distribution service companies. Retail companies with restricted product ranges and low cost profiles also found themselves in a stronger position.

It should be noted that regulatory controls are not only imposed by government. Often an industry itself may agree to restrict or control certain activities, e.g. after hours deliveries, which again must be examined from both points of view.

Competitive

Example: A new process enables a competitor to lower his unit costs, and therefore prices, by a significant amount
The threat is obvious enough but an opportunity does exist. A new process will undoubtedly require a major investment and consequently the risk to the innovator will increase. Thus, although his variable costs will be less, it is likely that overheads will show a significant increase and his break-even volume will increase as a consequence. If the market is growing the innovator may prosper but if the market is stable he will need to obtain the required volume from competitors. This will undoubtedly involve an increase in marketing expenditure which may result in the innovator being only marginally better off. The opportunity for his competitors is indirect and comes from the fact that in terms of opportunity cost the innovator is very likely to have forgone an opportunity to invest elsewhere.

The competitive factors in the position audit are likely to be mostly marketing oriented but financial and operational management considerations warrant equal weighting in the eventual analysis. Obviously, marketing factors will be given greater emphasis in a marketing position audit. It is the function of the corporate position audit both to highlight the broad factors and to focus the attention of management when conducting the marketing and distribution audits.

Technological

Example: The introduction of cage pallets
Technological change can cover a very broad spectrum. It ranges from major process changes, passing through raw material specification changes to unit load handling developments. An example of the latter has been the introduction of cage pallets* into grocery retailing in the UK. The impact

---

*Cage pallets are a development in which the unit designed to handle and transport goods in bulk from point of production to point of sale is also used as the point of sale unit. Under this system goods are placed in cage pallets at the point of production, price marked and remain in those pallets all the way to the point of sale.

17

of cage pallets has presented many grocery product manufacturers with board level policy problems concerning large volumes of business.

The opportunities (and threats) surrounding this particular change in technology are numerous. For the retailer there is an opportunity to effect considerable cost savings in both instore labour costs and inventory holding costs. For the manufacturer there may be fewer benefits and even increased costs. Large manufacturers may find the cage pallet difficult (and therefore costly) to incorporate into an existing production and distribution system. A small manufacturer may be more flexible and can do so without much effort. Furthermore the smaller manufacturer may see this service as an opportunity to increase his business with large customer outlets. Finally, the distribution service company may well regard the cage pallet as an opportunity to provide a cage pallet filling service at a cost which is attractive to both manufacturers and distributors.

It can be seen that the corporate position audit is very much a 'macro' approach. It should provide leads for both the subsequent marketing and distribution audits.

All planning must be based upon some assumption concerning the future of the internal and external environments. Thus we must consider *assumptions* next. Hussey [1] defines assumptions in corporate planning as 'a statement of opinion about the occurrence of an event which is outside the control of the planner'. As such they concern the external environment because internally the company should be able to control events. Assumptions provide two inputs to the planning process – they provide a foundation for developing plans and a co-ordinating effect. It is important that all aspects of the company's plans share common assumptions, failure to do so will result in incompatible plans.

Therefore, some of the assumptions made concern the state of the external environment. Therefore we need to consider the social, economic, technological, regulatory and, competitive elements comprising that environment. Whilst assumptions concerning these elements must be specific, they must also be sufficiently comprehensive to cover the needs of functional planners in the marketing, finance, manpower and operations management areas.

Concurrently the plan must begin to develop ideas on its *corporate mission* (or perhaps *missions*). The missions approach was discussed very briefly in the first chapter and the concept will be expanded here only in sufficient detail to enable this discussion to progress. A detailed treatment will be found in Chapter 3.

Many companies are primarily concerned with inputs (and their costs) into the production process. This is not to suggest that outputs are ignored but rather that priority is given to inputs. Budgets are traditionally set with an input orientation rather than an output orientation. Functional areas of the firm therefore work within a framework of budgets which relate to what they might spend within the budgeting period.

An alternative approach sees the firm as concerned primarily with creating outputs rather than with consuming inputs. The emphasis is placed upon customers and markets – and the outputs of the company need to satisfy customer needs and at the same time do so at a profit. There is nothing new conceptually here, indeed it is just an extension of the marketing concept of matching needs with resources. What is different is the approach to planning and resource allocation (i.e. budgeting).

The basic tenet of the missions approach is the attempt to answer the question: 'What business are we in?' Levitt [2] suggests that if the US railroads had thought to ask themselves this question some years ago and had answered: 'The transportation business', there would not have been the succession of financial crises that they have found themselves facing. As it was, many of the railroad companies saw their business as being 'railroads' – in itself too narrow a definition.

Other similar examples can be cited. The Hollywood film business took some time to come around to realising that they were in the entertainment business in the broadest sense, eventually making films for the 'arch enemy' television. One of the large data processing firms sees itself as being in the 'business efficiency' business. A manufacturer of disinfectants, cleansers and toilet tissues sees itself in the 'health' business. Finally, a camera and film manufacturer sees himself in the 'memories' business.

The activity of defining and establishing missions should not be the sole prerogative of the corporate planner. There are very good reasons why other activities should be involved and why their views on whether marketing, manufacturing or technological orientations be adopted. It will be shown later that when the missions approach is applied to distribution, four basic possibilities exist. We can use either product type, channel type, outlet type or service requirements as the criteria to define the mission. It will be seen that each has advantages based upon circumstances surrounding the business. What is important, and should be considered now is the need to think through the inter-relationships that exist and where possible give due consideration to the planning needs of the functional activities at subsequent levels.

The need is for areas of mutual interdependence to be established and reinforced. For example, it may be possible for very large companies to divisionalise their activities (e.g. ICI, Lyons) thereby facilitating the definition of missions at all levels. For others it is not so easy. Many

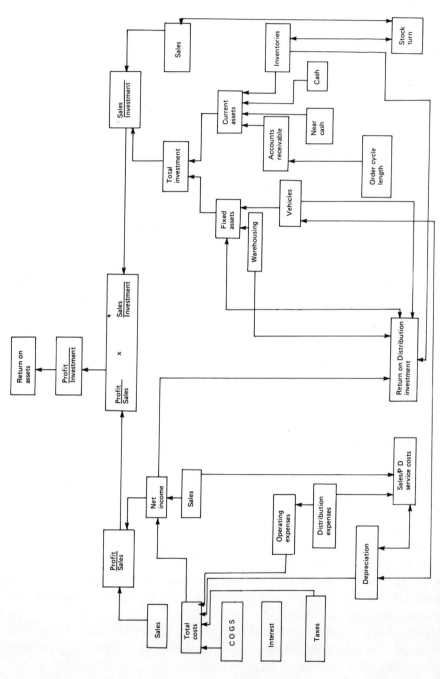

Figure 2.2   The influence of PDM on corporate performance

20

companies have added acquisitions (either companies or products) only to find that possible outlet or product synergy* potential fails to become fact.

Given the definition of the business the next step is to determine the overall objectives of the firm.

Corporate objectives are usually expressed as economic or non-economic. Examples of economic objectives are:

1 Return on equity.
2 Return on assets.
3 Growth in terms of sales or market share(s).
4 Risk reduction.
5 Gearing ratio debt/equity.
6 Cash flow.

Each objective has significance for PDM. Figure 2.2 illustrates the influence of PDM on corporate performance. It can be seen that it is vital that each objective is quantified because without this the system of planning and control cannot be applied. Various inter-relationships can be seen. For example, the stock turn figure reflects the efficient (or otherwise) use of inventory. Order cycle length has a direct influence on accounts receivable and warehousing and vehicles have indirect effects on asset use (and therefore replacement). The relationship between sales and distribution service costs and margins gives a measure of the revenue generating ability of the distribution system.

The non-economic objectives are concerned with:

1 Technological development.
2 Manpower development.
3 Environmental considerations.

Again each has implications for PDM. At virtually all levels of technological development PDM has an interest. An entirely new production process is likely to require changes within the existing distribution system, while technological development can take place within the distribution activity itself.

Management development programmes can only make distribution more effective. Management must be aware of, and take opportunity of, all advantageous policies in this sphere.

Much the same can be said for environmental considerations. Conservation, anti-noise, anti-pollution objectives each have obvious implications for distribution.

*Synergy being the so-called '2 + 2 = 5' effect.

Following the corporate objectives there must be corporate strategies. This subject was dealt with in some detail in the opening chapter. Here it is only necessary to consider the implications for PDM.

The reader will recall the Ansoff matrix introduced in the first chapter. There, certain strategies for business development were suggested each of which have implications for distribution planning.

Market penetration strategies require that sales of existing products are increased in existing markets. This may be achieved by pursuing an aggressive promotional programme but it may prove preferable to increase distribution service (which takes the competition more time to detect) in which case the pressures on the existing system will increase.

Product development (new products in existing markets) will require an additional investment in inventory holding, warehousing and delivery capability, with the possibility of a change in order cycle lengths. In certain instances new unitisation and handling methods may be necessary. Recently a company introduced a new grocery product but found that its distribution costs were considerably increased because the new product proved to be incompatible with the existing product range due to contamination problems when breakages occurred.

Market development strategies present physical distribution with another set of problems. These, it will be remembered, develop new markets for existing products. At the very least it is again clear that pressure will be put on existing facilities, together with the possibility of a need to develop an entirely new approach to the distribution service if the new customers desire differing service aspects from the existing customers.

Diversification clearly presents a number of problems. The company may well end the day with a totally incompatible product mix as far as distribution considerations are concerned. Thus diversification will undoubtedly provide the most problems in terms of distribution service. There are many examples of companies who have found that, far from lowering average costs, the demands of new customers for specific levels and types of service have been totally dysfunctional. One such company added a hospital equipment concern to its portfolio and found the products to be very expensive to handle and store within its own distribution activity and eventually resolved the problem by using outside facilities. The problems of merging distribution systems following corporate acquisitions can be so great that they could be the subject of a separate book!

The strategy formulation procedure described here is not as simple as it sounds. Often there is a great deal of activity attempting to find strategies which are within the company's resources. Where they can be met there remains the task of making the strategy explicit and pursuing the plan into the functional activities of the firm (Marketing, Operations, Finance and Manpower) by developing operational plans.

Summary

The relationship between PDM and corporate planning has been shown to be central to the core effective development of distribution strategies. A number of examples were used to show how the use of SWOT analysis (Strengths, Weaknesses, Opportunities, and Threats) can improve management's awareness of its current position and how it might change.

Finally the need was established for the company to formulate corporate objectives against which the role of distribution could be more clearly seen.

Notes

[1] D. Hussey, *Corporate Planning: Theory and Practice,* Pergamon, 1974.
[2] T. Levitt, 'Marketing Myopia', *Harvard Business Review,* July/August 1960.

3 Relating marketing planning to PDM

Introduction

We have discussed some of the major issues involved in the corporate planning process. In this chapter we will examine marketing planning and use the same perspective: both the component activities and their implications for PDM will be considered.

Marketing planning and its implications for PDM

The marketing planning process is charted in Figure 3.1. It does, of course, closely resemble the corporate planning process. However, the emphasis at this level of planning is on marketing detail.

The marketing plan starts with a marketing position audit. Firstly, some estimate of the positions reached by major products (or product groups) in terms of their product life cycles must be attempted. The product life cycle is a major diagnostic tool of product management and consequently of marketing planning. The concept is depicted in Figure 3.2.

During the period of introduction, the product's sales grow quite slowly and usually a loss rather than a profit is made. However, once the product becomes established and early users begin to repeat their purchases, promotion persuades other more cautious users to try the product and the rate of growth of sales increases. Usually, competitors seeing potential will imitate the product and add their weight to the promotional expenditure and accelerate the increase in the total sales of the product. No market opportunity is infinite and ultimately the rate of sales slows as the product moves into the maturity stage of the life cycle. Here there are few new sales to be obtained – repeat purchases from loyal customers and customers won from competitors are the only way in which an increase in sales may be achieved.

As the product reaches saturation there will normally be no further sales expansion unless the company modifies either product or price. Eventually, the product moves through to the decline stage of its life cycle, where despite remedial action sales decline continues, often dramatically.

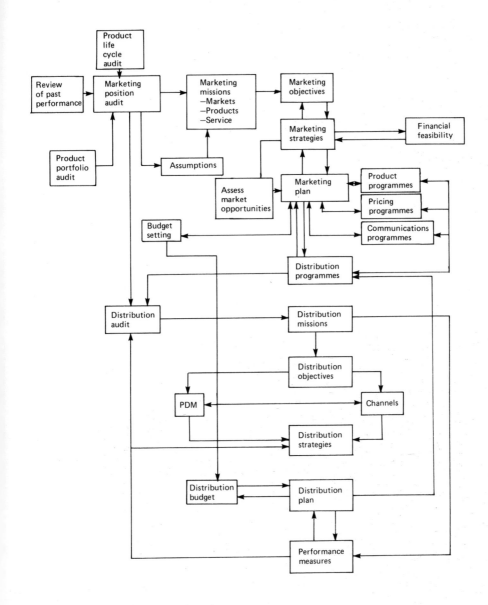

Figure 3.1 Marketing planning and distribution planning

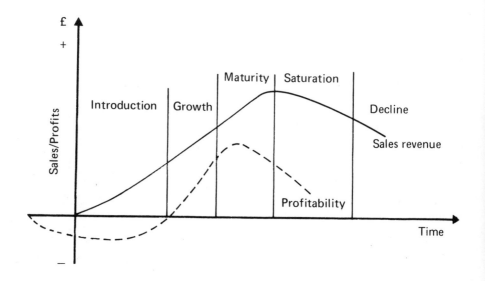

Figure 3.2 The product life cycle

Distribution policy can vary during the product life cycle. During the introduction stage the primary concern is usually to obtain consumer acceptance for the new product by creating consumer awareness of its existence, its functions and operating characteristics. Generally this is a slow, educative job, requiring a considerable amount of direct personal selling to the prospective customer. For both consumer and industrial products this calls for the shortest possible lines of communication between buyer and seller and maximum personal sales push to the consumer. For consumer goods this period is characterised by direct sales to exclusive or selected retailers, outlets capable of offering excellent service, working on relatively high margins and adhering to manufac-turer's recommended resale prices. For industrial products this period is usually marked by distribution either direct to customer or alternatively through franchised distributors, again of a high service character.

The growth phase usually involves a broadening of the market, which in turn generally requires a broadening of distribution channels to meet the needs of the increasing number of consumers. This frequently entails more

26

distributors. Personal sales effort and service remain high, and price is relatively stable, but control over outlets begins to weaken and outlets begin to compete with each other for business. This pattern intensifies in the maturity phase of the market. Price is a major marketing weapon with price wars becoming the norm. Mass distribution is the rule, with some of the older outlets beginning to drop out. Service declines noticeably.

Finally, during the decline stage, distribution is often confined to a few high volume/low price outlets. Distribution once more shifts to a direct to dealer pattern. Successful merchandising depends upon high turnover at relatively low percentage margins.

The implications of the product life cycle for physical distribution are very clear. Changes in outlet types and the emphasis on distribution service over the product life cycle should be ascertained. More importantly the life cycle stages for major products (or product groups) must be plotted in order that an appropriate level of service can be budgeted. As it has been shown, new products often require very high levels of service and availability. The costs of providing this can be prohibitive so service needs must be monitored throughout the product life cycle to ensure that the service offering is compatible with profit targets.

Changes in channels and outlets should also be appraised at this stage of the position audit. A company in the home decoration market missed an opportunity for large sales through supermarkets for some time because it was unaware of the changes that the environment had undergone.

Cash flow from products is another particularly important consideration. It follows from the product life cycle that products have varying requirements for funds. A recently introduced product is likely to need a considerable investment in promotion and in distribution service if it is to become a success. Conversely a declining product should be given a minimum of attention. Products at their maturity stages, with high market shares, should generate funds. By the time this situation has been reached there should no longer be a requirement for promotional investment and distribution service should have settled at an economic but competitive level.

If the product portfolio is balanced (i.e. it has a spread of products at differing stages in their life cycles) the company should be able to recycle its cash flows, i.e. use cash generated by the successful mature products to fund the new product and provide the financial support required to make them equally successful in the future.

A review of past performance should form a major part of the analysis, the object of which should be to take an overall view of the marketing operation with a view to identifying discrepancies and obvious irregularities. For instance, a beverage manufacturer found that one product group contained more than 50 variations of a basic product resulting in excessive inventory holding costs. Another example of the results of such a review is provided by a manufacturer of industrial cutting blades who was dismayed to find some 15 per cent of his products accounted for 90 per cent of his profits, the so-called 'Pareto effect'. During such a review a number of implications follow for PDM. In the examples above the problems produced by excessive inventory holding could be considerable. Furthermore, it is often found that the slower moving products generate more than a proportionate share of costs.

In this type of situation it usually follows that the Pareto effect also holds for customers, in other words something like 80 per cent of the company's sales come from only 20 per cent of the customers, with a similar split for costs.

In any planning situation ASSUMPTIONS must be made explicit. The specific need of marketing planners here is for assumptions that can be interpreted in marketing terms. Consider some likely social assumptions. These should express opinions based on sound evidence of likely continuing or developing trends in societal behaviour and attitude. Take the family as an example. Significant changes in size will have major impact for companies manufacturing staple products in such areas as food, beverages, clothing, etc. Likewise, changes in educational standards may result in a more discerning consumer able and determined to ensure that consumption objectives are maximised.

Distribution management is directly concerned with such changes. In the examples quoted here there are clear implications in terms of volume throughput, availability and service levels. At this juncture distribution managers should attempt to guide the marketing planners into developing a set of assumptions upon which sound distribution planning can be developed.

The concept of missions was discussed in the previous chapters. Here we shall explore their application to marketing planning. It is important that the needs of all marketing activities be considered in terms of facilitating marketing planning. We have established that we can use either product type, channel type, outlet type or service requirements as the criteria for the mission. But first there must be some clear definition of the businesses that company is in.

Immediately a problem can be seen. The company may define its business either too broadly or too narrowly. Clearly if the US railroads defined their mission as the transportation business they would imply that future growth areas may include airlines as potential acquisitions. In all likelihood this would prove disastrous because the management expertise required to run a large railroad is not guaranteed success when transferred to other such areas.

One suggestion for tackling the problem comes from Peter Ward [1] who suggests that it is:

> . . . convenient to sub-divide a company's overall identity into several such continuing areas of interest or dynamic product areas . . . Essentially a dynamic area defines a class of activities or products in functional or general terms. It should be broad enough to embrace a great number of product ideas including many that have not yet been conceived, but specific enough to be readily communicated and to focus a continuing review of product search.

Ward considers the word 'dynamic' is useful because it refers to technological dynamic equilibrium:

> As something leaves (becomes obsolete or uncompetitive), something else enters (is introduced) to take its place. Continuous product success (or expansion) is, therefore possible within an area.

This suggests two things. Firstly, dynamic product areas, or, missions, should as far as possible be timeless so that a company's activities may be capable of indefinite regeneration. Secondly, missions should only span a manageable width.

Ward continues with an example of mission definition:

> . . . an enormous range of products; pumps, compressors, auxiliary plant for ships and power stations, evaporators, valves and even houses. Within this range I discovered there were de-oilers and de-aerators . . . de-salination plant . . . arising from the company's flash evaporator work: water treatment plan, and an experimental pressure filter . . . The simple concept that embraced this miscellaneous collection of activities was 'equipment for materials separation'.

Thus the mission should bear relationship with the company's existing knowledge of technology, manufacturing facilities or market outlets. But it also needs the power to prompt new, relevant ideas, including those not yet invented or conceived. The mission, therefore, is based in the present but is future-oriented.

The concept of a mission owes its development to Robert McNamara who as Secretary of Defence in the US Administration developed a system of budgeting designated Planning-Programming-Budgeting-System

(PPBS) as a means of evaluating complex defence systems. The UK government has adopted it for some departments. For example, the Home Office is implementing this system of accounting into police forces. One item which caused surprise was the 'total' cost of police dogs. When all relevant costs are considered (i.e. wages of trainers and handlers and the cost of running dog vans, etc.) the result was startling. Under the conventional accounting system, the cost of police dogs was put at £1,600 by one force. The following year with the new accounting method, the cost in programme terms was shown to be £37,900!

The principle of PPBS (or Output Budgeting as it has come to be called) is that rather than budgets being determined functionally or departmentally they are set by first determining objectives for major missions, thus the emphasis is switched from inputs to outputs. The organisation recognises that the purpose of business is to create output rather than to consume inputs.

If we use the suggestions of Levitt and Ward we find that what in fact the company is doing is to analyse its activities in order to isolate those with a common thread. This thread may be defined in terms of technology, customer type, or some other common denominator.

Thus a food-grocery manufacturer may delineate the following missions. We sell to the public through a number of retail-wholesale institutions; we are, therefore, in the consumer service business. Some sales are made to hospitals and similar institutions requiring specific products and service; we are therefore, in the institutional service business. We also sell to hotels, restaurants and canteens; we are, therefore, in the catering business. We produce to individual customer product and packaging specifications; we are, therefore, in the own label business. These missions cut across conventional functional organisation charts. Figure 3.3a illustrates this principle.

The company will then set itself objectives for each mission and communicate these to the remainder of the organisation. Functional managers will be expected to assess their own participation in terms of the mission objectives and will consider alternative methods available to them by which they can achieve their own objectives. With this done the functional managers are then able to allocate resources to each mission and thus budgets are arrived at by a mission orientation. Figure 3.3b demonstrates this approach.

Business has successfully applied McNamara's PPBS. Smalter and Ruggles [2] give an account of the International Minerals and Chemicals Corporation installation of the system. IMCC identified some nine missions and the approach led IMCC management to conclude that its

30

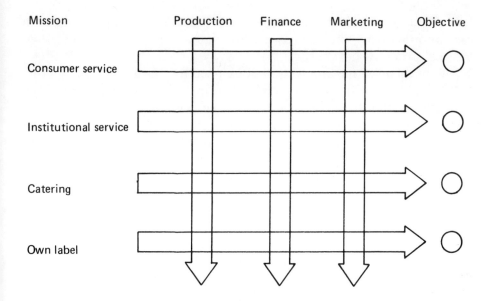

Figure 3.3a Missions cross conventional business organisational structures

(all figures in £'000)

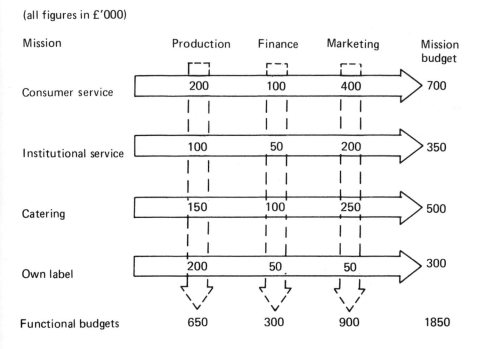

Mission	Production	Finance	Marketing	Mission budget
Consumer service	200	100	400	700
Institutional service	100	50	200	350
Catering	150	100	250	500
Own label	200	50	50	300
Functional budgets	650	300	900	1850

Figure 3.3b Output budgeting – budgeting on a mission basis

31

business must be oriented to the service of customers and that long term expansion must be directed more to the market environment and less to internal structure and skills.

The problem of mission width as discussed by Ward was dealt with by IMCC by categorising 'market missions' into three distinct groupings: agricultural, industrial and consumer. These groups were then further segmented, e.g. a foundry supplies mission was delineated within the industrial category. Other missions included plant nutrition, animal health and nutrition, oil well services, flavour enhancers, etc. IMCC found this perspective helped senior management to do a better job of sizing up possibilities for future growth. Thus the missions were defined with the need to bear a relationship with the company's existing knowledge of technology, manufacturing facilities, market outlet, etc.

IMCC use an annual profit plan combined with a five year programme plan. It was found that a complete resource and programme balance is difficult to attain, but that the missions approach identified areas of strength and areas of weakness. Possibly the greatest advantage which can be obtained is the facility of being able to match outputs and inputs against each other, the fact IMCC were not able to obtain a complete balance of resources/programmes is a minor disadvantage.

Given a clearly defined set of missions, these must be made specific in terms of marketing objectives. Objective setting is the basis or starting point for marketing planning. Marketing objectives will clearly reflect the previously defined corporate objectives but will break these down into more significant and meaningful terms. Marketing objectives provide the basis for marketing action and must therefore be measurable.

It will be recalled that in economic terms we could expect to see corporate objectives outlining such goals as return on assets, cash flow, risk reduction and so on. Based on these the marketing objectives could include:

1 Volume objectives.
2 Market share objectives.
3 Profit target after marketing costs.
4 Total market development growth.
5 Market segment(s) development growth.
6 Distribution coverage – total/segments.
7 Penetration of consumption units – total/segments, etc.

Given such marketing objectives as these what would be the implications for distribution planning?

Volume objectives have significance not only for physical distribution but for production planning and scheduling and financial planning in terms of cash flow and short term borrowing. They are vital for physical distribution planning as well. Volume throughput affects the planning of warehouse facilities and vehicle numbers and being able to forecast individual product volumes greatly facilitates specific planning.

Profit targets for marketing activities provide a basis for budgeting and reinvestment plans. They also enable the distribution manager to consider his service policies. Clearly lower margins imply lower service levels unless the projected sales volume is sufficiently high to provide the same or larger profit volumes.

Market and market segment growth objectives are again important. It may be asked why have a total market growth objective? For some companies whose interests reach across a number of differentiated markets there is often a situation whereby those interests (as indicated by market share) are such that specific efforts must be made to direct the development of the total market as well as their market shares in specified segments.

Distribution coverage and market penetration objectives have obvious interest for the distribution activity. Marked changes here can have serious impact on distribution service and therefore costs and as such are major planning considerations.

Summary

We have taken some time to introduce and discuss the general topic of planning and have in the preceding chapters worked from a general discussion and justification of planning, to consider the corporate plan and finally in this chapter have discussed marketing planning.

Distribution planning is as much a part of marketing planning as marketing planning is of corporate planning. Because of this relationship it is not really appropriate to deal with them in isolation. Indeed without a thorough prior understanding of the linkages the would-be user may well be left with an incomplete planning package.

Notes

[1] E. P. Ward, *The Dynamics of Planning*, Pergamon, 1970.
[2] D. J. Smalter and R. L. Ruggles, 'Six Business Lessons from the Pentagon', *Harvard Business Review*, March/April 1966.

4 Distribution planning and auditing: a systems approach

Introduction

The purpose of this chapter is to develop a systems approach for a corporate distribution planning and audit cycle. The 'systems approach' has become something of a jargon phrase in recent years. This is in some ways a pity as the philosophy behind it has much to offer management. Essentially, the systems approach implies an approach to problem solving which considers the whole rather than the parts, and tries to understand the nature of inter-relationship between those parts and their impact upon the whole. Taking a systems view in distribution planning, as we shall see, enables the planner to understand the total company wide impact of his proposals.

The need for a structured approach

By now it should be clear that any management activity requires careful planning and control to be effective. Furthermore, each activity must be co-ordinated both vertically and horizontally to ensure that complete system effectiveness is maximised. These three concepts of vertical and horizontal co-ordination and system effectiveness need further elaboration.

Firstly vertical co-ordination. The preceding chapters dealt with the development of corporate and marketing plans where the need for PDM to be considered at the development stages of each plan was stressed. There can be no benefit from a product development project for example, which overlooks either distribution channel problems or PDM considerations which could be significant in the success or failure of the project. These and similar problems can often be eliminated by incorporating vertical co-ordination in the planning process. Vertical co-ordination is a consultative process which enables the implications of a decision at one level in the company to be assessed in terms of their impact upon activities at other levels.

Equally, it is important that corporate activities are co-ordinated horizontally. Consider as an example the problems of relating salesmen's call cycles to deliveries. Clearly, both must be related to consumer purchasing frequencies and distributor ordering patterns. But as we have seen in previous chapters, the planning activities for these tasks are often performed in separate areas of the business. Thus it is essential that horizontal co-ordination is achieved so ensuring that one activity is not unintentionally planned to compromise another.

The third concept introduced above was that of system. A great deal has been written about systems, systems approaches, systems thinking and systems management. It must be a matter of regret that so much of the literature causes confusion in the minds of many readers. In a number of texts and articles, the term systems management is used to describe a computer based model. Others apply the concept to complicated flow charts which themselves often form the basis of computer applications.

These approaches miss the original point made by the systems protagonists: 'The basic notion of a system is simply that it is a set of interrelated parts' [1]. Seymour Tilles pointed to the lack of an overall company wide approach in decisions taken within a single functional area of the firm. He suggested that the firm is not just a 'social system' nor is it a 'data processing system' nor can it be described as a 'system of funds flows'. He contends that these specific approaches must be synthesised if a worthwhile approach is to be found. The answer he suggests is offered by systems theory whereby:

1   The company is defined as system within which other 'subsystems' operate.
2   System objectives can be established and performance criteria set.
3   Subsystems are identified and created.
4   The 'total' system is integrated to achieve stated objectives.

In the context of the wider environment the system of the firm itself becomes a subsystem within the environment in which it operates and likewise within the operating functions of marketing, production, finance, manpower and distribution.

To ensure that the company's overall objectives are met rather than those of the individual function, strict control of the firm is necessary. Examples of the type of problems that can arise when each activity is given its head can be seen in Figure 4.1.

Figure 4.1 represents a series of situations any one of which could obtain within a company. While they are of course hypothetical, they demonstrate the principle of how it is possible for the firm to operate at a sub-optimal level due to the fact that inter-functional conflict exists and is

Subsystems goal	Purchasing	Production	Marketing	Finance	Logistics
Bulk purchases of materials	Advantage: larger discounts		Disadvantage: working capital tied up		Disadvantage: warehousing costs increased
Long production runs		Advantage: low costs	Disadvantage: working capital tied up	Disadvantage: narrow product range	Disadvantage: warehousing costs increased
Broad product range	Disadvantage: discounts small on low volume purchases	Disadvantage: short, high cost runs	Disadvantage: finished goods stocks high	Advantage: more sales through wider customer appeal	Disadvantage: higher costs through more administration and more warehousing space
Tighter credit control			Advantage: greater use of working capital	Disadvantage: possible loss of sales	
4 day delivery (from seven days)			Disadvantage: higher operating costs	Advantage: more sales because of better service	Disadvantage: system costs increased in order to meet service requirements
Unit loads		Advantage: lower operating costs	Disadvantage: loss of sales to small customers		Advantage: system costs can be lowered by eliminating uneconomic calls

Figure 4.1 Situations which can give rise to inter-departmental conflicts—micro subsystems

not resolved. Each situation is reversible (i.e., in the first situation the finance and logistics managers would consider small purchase volumes ideal but the purchasing manager would not because he would then lose on bulk discounts, and from increased handling and ordering costs).

These conflicts can be resolved but not easily. Clearly in the first case it is possible mathematically to calculate an economic order quantity which will take account of the costs and other interests of all parties. This example seeks to make a simple point: the systems approach to management involves a recognition that any organisation is a system made up of individual units, each unit having its own goals. Management must be aware that, if the company is to reach its overall goals, it can do so only by considering the entire system and seeking to understand and define the interrelationships, and then to integrate them in a manner which enables the organisation to pursue its goals effectively.

Inevitably, this means that some functional units within the organisation may not achieve their own objectives. What is considered best for the whole system is not necessarily best for each component. This is the concept of sub-optimisation, a process whereby the parts may each need to operate at a less-than-optimal level in order that the whole may be optimised.

Parallel to this concept is that of the 'trade off'. A trade off situation arises when a decision taken in one functional area of the firm which might affect that area's costs or effectiveness is balanced against the effects of that same decision on the other functional areas of the firm. Thus a decision might be taken to centralise warehousing which will not only affect the costs of warehousing but also the costs of transport and the costs of inventory investment. Likewise, total system effectiveness may also be affected.

The conventional view of business operations is that they take place in several clearly delineated centres (often defined as cost centres for budgeting purposes). A total operation based upon a systems approach offers a more efficient alternative to overall operations management; for while there are numerous techniques and methods by which each of the functional centres may operate more efficiently, they are sub optimal unless they consider the interaction of the areas with one another. Therefore, if the company wishes to minimise total operating costs, a correct balance between centres must be found. The total cost approach recognises that it may be necessary to increase costs in one area of the business to effect an overall reduction of costs for the business as a whole and thereby increase total profitability.

Closely associated with the total approach to system management is the methodology of systems analysis. One writer on this topic, Quade [2], suggests that systems analysis is a process of evaluation. He suggests the process has five elements:

1 *The objective.* Because systems analysis is undertaken primarily to help choose a policy or cause of action, the first and most important task is to discover what the decision maker's objectives are, and then the extent to which these objectives are achieved by various alternatives may be measured. This done, strategies and policies can be examined, compared and recommended on the basis of how well (or cheaply) they can accomplish these objectives.
2 *The alternatives.* These are the means by which it is hoped the objectives can be attained. They may be policies or strategies and need not be obvious substitutes for each other.
3 *The costs.* The choice of a particular alternative for accomplishing the objectives implies that certain specific resources can no longer be used for other purposes. While these can be measured in money terms, they are of course opportunity costs, i.e., the benefits that could have been obtained if the resources had been utilised elsewhere.
4 *Models.* These represent, in a simplified manner, the cause and effect relationships implicit in the systems under study. Models may be verbal, graphical, mathematical, or even mechanical. In systems analysis, the purpose of a model is to estimate the costs that would be incurred for each alternative and the extent to which the objectives would be attained.
5 *A criterion.* A rule or standard against which the alternatives may be taken in order of desirability. It provides a means for weighing cost against effectiveness.

Systems analysis takes place in three over-lapping stages. In the first, the formulation stage, issues are clarified, the extent of the inquiry limited and elements identified. In the second stage, the search stage, information is gathered and alternatives generated. The third stage is analysis.

To evaluate say a distribution system design, the various alternatives are examined by means of the model(s). For example, a complete market can be simulated on a computer, with product flows, customer service requirements, depot location alternatives, inventory service levels and transportation mode alternatives forming data inputs*. Such models may be used to evaluate the impact of alternative systems on market share and hence revenue and profits. A simpler example is the mechanical analogue

---

*See for example the model described by D. J. Bowersox, et al., in 'Physical Distribution Planning with Simulation', *International Journal of Physical Distribution*, October 1971.

approach to depot location in which weights are used to simulate levels of demand.

In each case the model will tell us what consequences or outcomes can be expected from each alternative, i.e. what the costs are and to what extent each objective is attained. A criterion is then used to weigh the costs against effectiveness and thereby enable the alternatives to be ranked. In the first example, given in the previous paragraph, market share may be one measure used. Others may be customer service performance or possibly budgeted cost levels. In the second example costs could be used but so too could product throughput, vehicle and/or warehouse utilisation levels.

This discussion leads us to the final aspect of the systems analysis process: cost effectiveness. Cost effectiveness analysis has been defined as: 'a technique for choosing among *given* alternative courses of action in terms of their cost and their effectiveness in the attainment of specified objectives'[3].

There are of course a set of basic requirements to enable a meaningful analysis to be performed. The analyst needs:

(a)   a specific statement of objectives;
(b)   a complete list of alternatives to be considered;

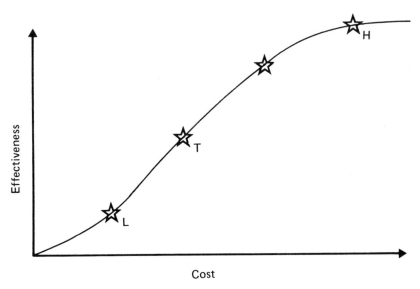

Figure 4.2   A cost effectiveness curve showing the changing relationship between increases in cost and corresponding increases in effectiveness

(c) acceptable measures of effectiveness;
(d) acceptable measures of costs.

Cost effectiveness analysis is rooted in micro-economic theory, specifically, the 'Law of Diminishing Returns', which concludes: 'Generally increases in some inputs relative to other fixed inputs will eventually increase the total output *less than proportionally* to the increase in inputs'.

Therefore additional output derived from a given input diminishes and Figure 4.2 illustrates the principle. Typically, the relationship can be represented by an s-shaped curve: up to point L the increase in resource allocated has a less than proportionate effect upon effectiveness. Between L and T an increase in resources (and therefore costs) brings about a more than proportional increase in effectiveness. Beyond T the rate of increase progressively decreases such that approaching H the marginal returns decrease rapidly so as to make further investment in resources questionable.

Choosing appropriate measures of effectiveness is probably the most difficult aspect of cost effectiveness analysis. The two characteristics seemingly most appropriate to the analysis are often in conflict. First of all, measures should be relevant and second, they should be measurable. The

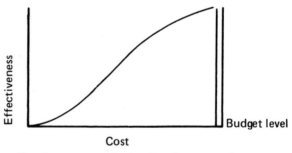

Figure 4.3a Cost-effectiveness analysis: fixed approach cost

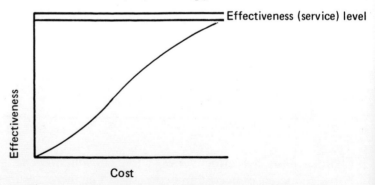

Figure 4.3b Cost-effectiveness analysis: fixed effectiveness approach

40

conflict occurs because the most relevant are often very difficult to measure and vice-versa.

Other problems exist. The choice between fixed cost and fixed effectiveness approaches is a pre-requisite in all cost effectiveness analysis. Both approaches have merits, liabilities and relevance. Both are illustrated in Figure 4.3. The fixed cost approach is often favoured because of its closer association to operational management in the form of budgets and standard costs; whereas a fixed effectiveness approach would be suitable when minimum performance requirements such as service levels must be met. The former approach would attempt to maximise output from a given level of input whilst the latter attempts to achieve a required level of output for minimum input.

This brief summary of systems management and analysis techniques is adequate at this stage to develop our approach to distribution planning and control. We shall need to return to systems thinking later in this chapter. However, before outlining the distribution planning/control model to be used in this text some discussion concerning the relationship between service and demand will prove worthwhile.

The relationship between service and demand

There can be no doubt that distribution service is related to sales. If it were not there would be no justification for companies to run expensive distribution systems. Similarly, there can be no doubt that the provision of distribution service costs money. Indeed we can be more sure of the effects of improved service levels on costs than we can about its effect on sales. In some cases improved service may not be reflected in improved sales.

However, it is not all black. Increased service in many cases has meant increased profits. Research by Hutchinson and Stolle [4] found that:

> Intelligent investments in customer service can pay off handsomely, as the following testimonies indicate:
> 1 Supplier to the oil industry – 'we attribute a 5 per cent increase in sales directly to the improved delivery service and reduced number of stock shortages we achieved several months ago'.
> 2 Tool manufacturer – 'The use of air freight gave us the distribution 'plus' we needed to successfully enter the consumer market'.
> 3 Food manufacturer – 'Determination of our customers' *real* service requirements led to the redesign of our entire distribution system at a saving of $2 million annually'.

41

While each of these companies obviously has taken a different tack in the management of customer service, all three have pursued courses with certain characteristics in common. Each has made a quantitative evaluation of service. Each has considered service from the customer's viewpoint. Each has evaluated the service provided by competition.

Customer service can be shown to be an important aspect of physical distribution planning. Service may feature as a basis for setting distribution objectives or for defining distribution missions. Just how depends upon product, customer or competitive factors and is a subject which will be discussed in later chapters.

Obviously, service is more critical for some companies than for others and it should be the first task to determine whether service is an important factor influencing demand. Each industry (and each company within that industry) has individual service requirements but there are some common factors which indicate whether or not the industry is sensitive in its response to service:

1 *Product substitutability.* If a customer has no particular brand loyalty and willingly accepts a competitive product offered by a retailer, it is clear that minimisation of stock outs at the retail level is essential if the manufacturer is to be profitable.
2 *Product criticality.* For some industrial companies the cost of a stock out can be enormous, e.g. in the motor industry assembly lines can be stopped because of the lack of an assembly part. In such an instance delivery reliability is absolutely essential.
3 *Complementary products.* There are some products which, if absent on outlets' shelves, will restrict the sale of a complementary product. In such cases the combined sales may represent a considerable proportion of the outlets revenue. Again service is crucial.
4 *The cost of customer enquiries.* If these represent an unacceptable proportion of salesmen's and sales administration's time there is a clear indication that service is of concern to the enquiring companies.

Once a customer is found to be 'service sensitive' a supplier should capitalise on this and provide a level of service that will prove mutually beneficial to both companies. This requires the supplier to consider the impact of his service on his customers' profitability as well as his own.

The benefits of improved service to a customer can take many forms. For example:

1 *A lowering of inventory holding costs.* Improved delivery reliability allows the retailer to reduce his safety stocks.
2 *Fewer lost sales due to retailer stockouts.* If a product is not on the shelf there are five possibilities open to the consumer:
(a) buy same brand, another size – in which case the retailer may gain (or lose) revenue;
(b) buy a competitive brand – brand switching is a loss of business for the supplier;
(c) forgo the purchase – which results in temporary loss of business for both supplier and distributor;
(d) purchase the product elsewhere – store switching is a loss of business for the retailer;
(e) purchase an item from an entirely different product group – both supplier and retailer may lose.
3 *Better production planning.* The customer is himself able to avoid line shut downs and improve his own delivery times and reliability which means a double benefit of cost savings and increased sales.
4 *Competitive advantages specific to certain industries or companies.* Better service may invoke particular responses from individual firms and industries, e.g. if a company's usual supplier is unable to meet his order, within a certain time period, he may divert this (and subsequent) order to an alternative supply source which can offer faster and more reliable delivery.

There are naturally benefits to companies who consider their customers' point of view regarding service. Such benefits could include:

1 In return for providing the retailer with a high level of availability from stock the distributor might expect to obtain a share of his competitor's business and an increase in display as and when the retailer reduces his purchases from his other suppliers.
2 The reduction in retail stock outs means a reduction in a supplier's share of lost sales.
3 The increased profitability for the customer will increase his dependence and therefore business with his service minded supplier.

By now it is clear that customer service is an important ingredient in determining profitability. Equally important is the need to determine just what customers require in terms of service. It should not be assumed that all customer service requirements are the same. It is possible, but by no means certain, that customers within a specified category have similar needs. This should never be taken for granted: it is essential that individual needs be considered during the planning activity. These involve an audit of current needs and appropriate performance controls to measure and monitor subsequent service offering.

Systems analysis in PDM

Earlier the systems approaches of Tilles and Quade were discussed. We now need to become more specific and to apply this work in the context of PDM. To do this we can enlist further views, those of Jenkins [5], who extends the systems approach beyond the activities we have discussed. Jenkins considers that a systems approach includes problem formulation, project organisation, system definition (inter-system relationships in addition to intra-system relationships), information and data sources and collection, and includes Quade's requirements of objectives, alternatives and effectiveness measures.

The systems analysis approach as defined by Jenkins proceeds as follows:

Formulation of the problem. What is the problem? How did it arise? Who sees it as important? Why is it important? Is this the real problem or are the features just symptoms of a more fundamental problem? Will it save (make) money?

Organisation of the project. What is the best composition for the systems team? Are its terms sufficiently wide? When is the project to be completed? Has a preliminary project schedule been constructed? Have duties been allocated so that a more detailed critical path schedule can be set up?

Definition of the wider system. What is the environment in which the system will have to operate? How does the local system fit into the wider system?

What are the objectives of the wider system? Have competitive and senior systems been properly taken into account? How do they influence the objectives of the local system under study? Is there a danger of sub-optimisation?

What are the objectives of the local system? Have a list of objectives, in order of importance, been drawn up? Have the constraints been identified? Are there some subjective features which are difficult to quantify? Have the objectives been agreed? Have they been communicated to system members?

Have the measures of effectiveness been identified? Have conflicting objectives been properly weighed? Are the effectiveness measures

44

relevant? Are they measurable? How many criteria are there? What method is to be used to 'weight' these decision criteria in terms of relative importance?

Have all sources of information been identified? Have all important persons and sources of data been contacted? Has all relevant data been assembled and presented in the most appropriate way?

Have all the alternatives been identified? Is the local system the best system? Are alternative configurations more effective at the same levels of cost; just as effective at lower levels of cost?

This approach to systems analysis can be readily adapted for use within the context of PDM. Using this approach can prevent the all too frequent occurrence of failing to identify the real problem. Often a symptom of the problem is tackled only to discover later that the real cause lies elsewhere.

Thus a company might identify a distribution problem in that cost per ton handled in their central warehouse has steadily increased in the last two years. Traditional approaches to problem solving might have directed attention to the introduction of more efficient handling devices to keep operating costs down. In fact the real problem may have lain within the wider system, for example, the product mix of the company may have changed considerably, let us say through the introduction of less dense (i.e. volume/weight ratio) products. Therefore cost/ton would be a misleading figure by itself: cost/volume unit would be more appropriate and might even show a decline.

The crucial role of feedback

If we view the distribution activity of the company in systems terms then it is possible to see distribution decisions as an 'input' to the system and the impact of those decisions on revenue and costs as the 'output' of the system [6]. The 'process' whereby these inputs are converted into outputs represents the logistics system of the company. The effectiveness of the system can therefore be seen in terms of the ratio of outputs to inputs. This ratio will be affected not only by the way the system is organised, but also by the effects of external variables, in the language of systems these are 'restrictions'. Finally, in order that the system can achieve the objectives set for it there must be some means of relating the output to the input, i.e. a means of measuring, not controlling, performance. This element of the system is termed 'feedback'. This concept of a system is summarised in Figure 4.4.

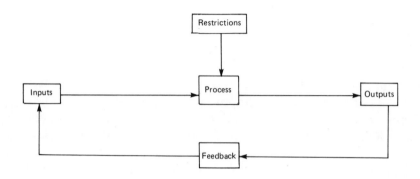

Figure 4.4 The systems concept

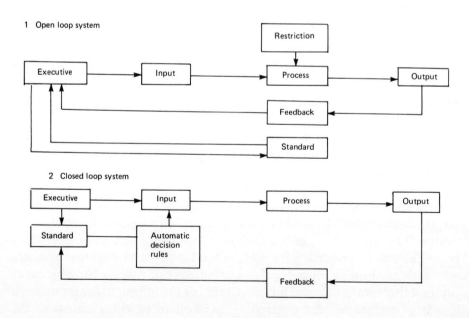

Figure 4.5 System types

The extent to which the system will be self regulating will depend upon how the feedback element is related to the inputs. If, for example, the feedback is in the form of regular reports on order cycle lead-times, service levels and so on, then management is required to base judgements on this data and take corrective action where necessary – either by adjusting the inputs or by making changes to the process. On the other hand it may be possible for management to stipulate a number of decision rules such as: 'If the rate of growth of demand exceeds a certain level then increase safety stock holding by such a level'. This type of self regulating system is exactly analogous to the thermostat on a room heater. The first type of system identified above, i.e. that requiring managerial intervention, is termed 'open loop' while the latter type is a 'closed loop' system. The differences are demonstrated in Figure 4.5.

It will be clear that only the simplest of logistics activities are capable of being controlled via a closed loop system. Because of the large number of variables involved in the assessment of logistics performance and the constant change of circumstances surrounding that performance, each deviation of performance from the planned level requires executive judgement. Therefore, the closed loop type of system is generally limited to such areas as inventory control where it is feasible to prescribe decision rules to enable the system to become self adjusting.

In reality, the type of monitoring and control system that is feasible tends to be a combination of the two. Executive intervention in the system is made wherever the monitor reports 'exceptional' circumstances. If, for example, replenishment levels are determined automatically it is still possible for a 'management by exception' approach to be used when, for example, the monitor reports a sudden, unexpected change in demand.

Summary

The need for a systems approach to the examination of distribution policies and plans has been emphasised in this chapter. The concept of the 'trade off' was introduced and it was suggested that the successful identification of trade offs within the distribution activity has been at the heart of effective distribution management.

The role of cost effectiveness analysis in distribution planning was experienced and in this context the relationship between distribution service and demand was emphasised.

Finally, the systems concept of 'feedback' was highlighted as the means whereby the distribution planning procedure could be controlled in the light of performance.

Notes

[1] S. Tilles, 'The Manager's Job: A Systems Approach', *Harvard Business Review,* January/February 1963.
[2] E. S. Quade, 'Systems Analysis Techniques for Planning – Programming – Budgeting', P.3322, RAND Corporation, March 1966.
[3] B. G. King, 'Cost-Effectiveness Analysis: Implications for Accountants', *Journal of Accountancy,* March 1970.
[4] W. M. Hutchinson and J. F. Stolle, 'How to Manage Customer Service', *Harvard Business Review,* November/December 1968.
[5] G. M. Jenkins, 'The Systems Approach', *Journal of Systems Engineering,* 2(1), 1970.
[6] M. G. Christopher, 'The New Science of Logistics Systems Engineering', *International Journal of Physical Distribution,* Vol. 2, No. 1, 1971.

5 The distribution audit

Introduction

The audit is probably the most important feature of the distribution planning and control process. In the operations, planning and control cycle of any activity an integral element is the audit or the appraisal of the existing situation or position, both in terms of the external environment and the internal operating environment of the company. Referring back to Figure 1.1 (page 3), the audit is essentially a device for monitoring these environments and for providing an answer to the question: 'Where are we now?'

Unlike the traditional accounting audit which occurs at regular intervals, usually annually, the distribution audit must operate on a more continuous basis, to provide a monitor on these environments. These environmental profiles must be continually maintained if the company's PDM strategy is to respond appropriately to change, or if new strategies are to be evaluated in terms of existing capability and constraints.

The Distribution Audit is conducted at two levels. At a micro level it is concerned with questions of resources, capacities, cost profiles and volume throughput. The macro level is concerned with market needs, competition, technology, regulatory changes, etc.

The audit poses practical problems; in many cases it requires the structuring of information gathering systems specifically designed to generate data for the audit. Once installed the information system must be capable of continuous updating and be able to provide a response, if not in real time then in time for decisions to be made effectively. Many companies who conduct position audits as part of their corporate planning activities find that the ongoing monitor is, in fact, provided as a by product of an existing management information system. It makes sense to think along similar lines when the PDM monitor is being designed – a PDM system requires information to function and it requires a monitor to survive.

The macro and micro levels are not discrete, they overlap within the audit activity. For example, data concerning internal and external attitudes towards PDM technology and conceptual developments are equally important in the audit because it indicates likely progress within the company's industry and those of its suppliers and customers: a trend

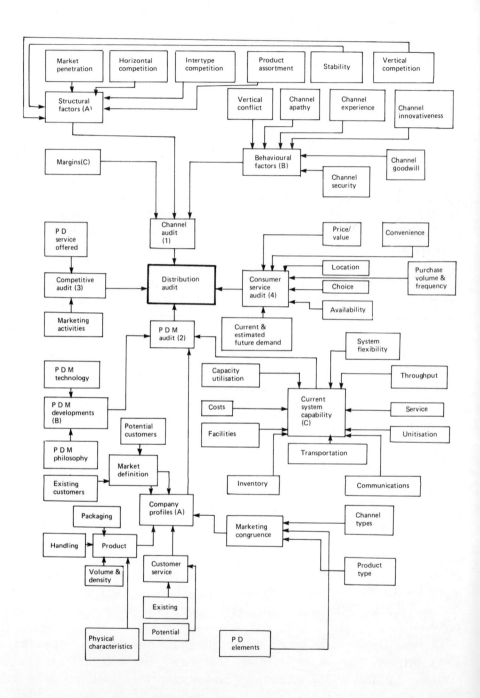

Figure 5.1   The distribution audit

towards a particular form of packaging may offer an opportunity to provide a new service to customers or possibly to lower costs if handled appropriately.

Not surprisingly, perhaps, the distribution audit is a complex procedure reaching out across, and beyond the company, to gather and relate data on system performance and effectiveness. Figure 5.1 summarises the multiplexity of considerations that need to be brought together in the auditing process and reference to this Figure will aid the understanding of the following discussion. Let us now consider some of these elements in detail under the headings of the four major components of the distribution audit: The channel audit; the PDM audit; the competitive audit and the customer service audit.

1   The channel audit

The marketing channel (or distribution channel) can be defined as the course taken in the transfer of title to a commodity. It is necessary to consider both the route of exchange (and its administrative and financial control) and the physical movement of the product from its original source of supply (taking into account changes of form) to its ultimate consumption. Thus channel decisions include:

1   A choice of intermediary.
2   A consideration of the physical distribution implications of the alternative intermediaries.
3   The margins available.

A channel audit will enable the channel member to ascertain:

1   Congruence of objectives:
    (a)   supplier's objectives;
    (b)   distributor's objectives;
    (c)   consumers' objectives.
2   A profile of behavioural factors.
3   The need, if any, to make changes in:
    (a)   his own objectives;
    (b)   the control factors.

There are three main elements of the channel audit – an analysis of structural factors, an analysis of behavioural factors and an analysis of margins.

A Structural factors

Structural factors relate to the capability of the channel to perform in the way we need it to if company channel objectives are to be achieved. Such channel objectives might include:

1 Market/segment share.
2 Profit/contribution.
3 Return on channel investment.
4 Channel member allegiance.
5 Outlet penetration.
6 User penetration.

Any intermediaries in the channel will also have objectives. For example:
Profit/contribution;
inventory turnover rates and return on investment.

For both effectively to meet the consumers' objectives which might be primarily: choice convenience availability and value for money, there has to be supplier/distributor co-operation in the form of agreement by each to undertake a number of activities. For example, the manufacturer will expect of the distributor:

1 Inventory carrying support – product width, product depth and location.
2 Market development activities.
3 Market intelligence.

The distributor will expect support from the manufacturer in terms of:

1 Credit.
2 Promotion allowances.
3 Market development.
4 Market intelligence.

(Figure 5.1 links these and demonstrates their interdependence.)

Those structural factors seemingly most important in this vein are summarised:

Market penetration. The share of business in each of the major channel, outlet and consumer group serviced by the company in terms of sales and profitability.
Horizontal competition. A measure of the extent of competition between outlet types in terms of ownership, e.g. in food – Sainsbury v. Tesco v. Fine Fare. For consumer durables – Curry v. Lloyd v. Rumbelow. This is an

important aspect of the channel audit because it gives the supplier an indication of the amount of competition there is for consumer expenditure and the amount of power that the retail outlets wield. The fewer the outlets the more powerful they are and the greater their demand for discounts and service are likely to be. Probably the most useful measure is a form of concentration ratio, showing the number of distributor companies and their share of total business and total outlets.

Inter type competition. A measure of the different type of store operating in the channel, e.g. the discounter v. selected product promotions operation. Again this is useful and necessary information because a wide variety of distributor philosophies probably signifies an equally wide set of demands (differing demands) for customer service. And again, measurement is probably best handled by concentration ratios similar to those outlined above.

Product assortment. Two distributor measures are of use. The first is the width of the distributor's product range from two points of view. Does the distributor stock complementary and/or competitive products? Do those products stocked emit the image of our own products? The second consideration concerns product range depth. Here the concern is whether or not the distributor is capable of providing (or willing to give) the levels of service, or product availability, seen as necessary for consumer/customer service by the manufacturer/supplier.

Stability. Channel stability comprises a number of aspects. Firstly, and most important, does the channel have a high number of entries and exits? In other words does the channel appear to be offering intermediaries sufficient returns for their efforts? Secondly, the volume of business should be examined for growth trends (or decline) and for inexplicable fluctuations. Thirdly, the channel should be examined in terms of stability of margins and service requirements. Changes are obviously likely to happen and should be sought and be welcomed provided they are mutually acceptable. However, persistent demands for ever increasing discounts and levels of service can eventually lead to serious problems. These trends should be monitored.

Vertical competition. In many industries there are widely differing approaches to channel structure. Often there is considerable vertical integration in a channel brought about by the competition for the consumer's disposable income and for the limited access to the consumer. Integration can therefore be forward (as described) or backward to secure sources of supply. An indication of the level of vertical competition will be made clear by the 'degree of directness' within the channel, usually by the number of intermediaries in each significant channel.

B Behavioural factors

A marketing channel is composed of a series of intermediaries, each, as we have seen, having individual sets of objectives. It is important that the relationships between them (behavioural relationships) be identified and monitored on a regular basis. These factors are of equal importance as the structural factors previously discussed, for without good working relationships between (and among) channel members the channel will not remain as an efficient unit for very long. Some of the important behavioural factors are:

Vertical conflict. There are two potential areas for vertical conflict – price and non-price. Price conflict concerns the problems between supplier and distributor price and margins policies. Price conflict is more likely to occur when dealing with a wide range of distributor 'types'; a discounter's pricing policy may be seen as incompatible with his supplier's product image. Conflict concerning margins is likely to occur at all levels of distribution.

Channel apathy. The willingness of the channel (or of individual members) to respond to internal or external changes or demands such as intensified competition from an alternative channel structure or, perhaps, an attempt by a manufacturer to develop his business through new product introductions.

Channel experience. Channel member's experience in handling products and operating in specific markets enables them to build expertise in these areas. Their experience as actual channel members is important to monitor particularly when channel changes are under consideration or, possibly, new products.

Channel innovativeness. The innovativeness of the channel reflects its attitude towards risk. It can also be viewed as the entrepreneurial flair of the channel. Thus the attitudes of channel members towards new products, changing channel tasks and distribution method, are important to know and to monitor when supplier initiated changes are being considered. If monitored regularly the most appropriate time for change can be chosen.

Channel goodwill. The extent to which channel members co-operate with each other and with the market in order to maintain social stability within the channel system is a measure of channel goodwill. A useful measure which indicates their willingness to co-operate in times of short supply in a joint attempt at putting the end user to a minimum of inconvenience.

Channel security. There are three measures worthy of consideration. Commercial security applies to the relationship between supplier and distributor in the field of product development and test marketing. Changes to physical distribution service would fall into this area, particularly when a new service package is being tested. Security of supply is often an important aspect of supplier/distributor relationships. It is twofold inasmuch that the supplier also seeks security of access to consumer markets. The third aspect concerns the security of service to end users, an aspect of vital importance to capital goods and consumer durables.

C   Margin

Channel margins should be considered against the value added by intermediaries. Usually, it is assumed that the intermediary 'adds value' or enhances the profitability of his suppliers' operation either by reducing costs in certain activity centres due to scale effects, e.g., sales calls, physical distribution (inventory holding, transportation, etc.) or, by carrying out certain functions on behalf of the supplier. Suppliers can either pay directly for these benefits (in the form of discounts) or indirectly (in the form of services). Services usually include promotion, advice on product range, credit, site location advice and general consultancy services.

The composition of discount/service package usually is the result of a round of negotiations between supplier and distributor and is based upon a mutually beneficial understanding of each other's business objectives.

2   The PDM audit

This element of the distribution audit has three main components: the company profile; PDM developments and current system capability.

A   Company profiles

Product profile. Analysing the product with an emphasis on those aspects with direct relevance to PDM enables the distribution planner to seek specific indications of current and future areas requiring attention in system planning.

Packaging is a basic concern because the promotional, protective and size considerations each play a major role in system design. Current merchandising trends favour the package as a sales instrument and this must be recognised. Equally, persistent monitoring will show emergent trends.

Handling costs are dependent upon the physical characteristics of each product, determining the range of storage and transportation alternatives available for consideration. Special handling of products can be necessitated by size or perishable features and a regular review is necessary. The volume of individual products is important from two points of view. Firstly, the number of items has an obvious direct relationship with distribution costs. Secondly, the rate of flow of products throughout the year must be monitored and seasonal variations investigated or planned for. Similarly, the density of the product mix (i.e. the volume/weight ratio) will need to be monitored, affecting as it does the economics of corporate distribution.

Customer service performance with existing customers should be monitored. Specifically the following:

1   Availability.
2   Delivery.
3   Delivery reliability.
4   Order processing and progressing.
5   Picking errors.
6   Back order procedures.
7   Returned goods.

A useful cross reference is the correlation of market share with customer service levels.

Market profile

The market profile should attempt to quantify current and potential customer demand for individual products by determining:

1   Who the customers are – existing and potential.
2   How much they buy.
3   How much they are likely to buy.
4   What physical distribution services they require.
5   Where they are located and where deliveries would be made.

Each item of information represents basic input for physical distribution planning. Service and location considerations are of obvious importance. New service requirements may be far too expensive to contemplate on a regular basis, while a new customer requiring branch deliveries to 1,000 stores nationally distributed could well pose insurmountable problems in terms of current capability. Volumes too have significance: an increase in volume throughput caused by the addition of a new and large customer may affect operational efficiency and in so doing lower service standards totally.

Any company with a multi-product range must consider the problems of marketing congruence. Three main considerations apply. Firstly, the need to view the multiplicity of channels that may need to be managed. Often the management problems are such that management effectiveness can be rapidly diluted as the number of channels increases. Often it is more profitable to restrict the company's expansion if it is known that to do so will result in a sub-optimal profit situation. The fundamental cause is, of course, the differential needs for service and the expense involved in ensuring that the multiplicity of standards are established, monitored and maintained.

The second consideration is product congruence. An expanding company is required to offer a broad product range with many product pack size and flavour varieties. This adds, once again, to the management problem.

Thirdly, as a consequence of broadening operations there is the risk that physical distribution philosophy and technology will differ widely among suppliers and distributors. An example may be the packaging and unitisation specifications that new/prospective customers often require, adding a great deal to costs.

B PDM developments

The distribution audit must of necessity include a review of the physical distribution activity itself. This review can be broken down into two clear segments. First PDM technology must be monitored for cost saving/revenue generating applications that are capable of incorporation into the corporate physical distribution system. Thus a review of current and likely future developments in key areas to the company must be part of the audit. Likely topics include – transportation, warehousing/handling, order processing and progressing communications and unitisation. In addition two major questions must be answered: 'Who initiates change: suppliers or distributors?' and 'What have been recent implications of change?'

PDM philosophy developments need close scrutiny and a number of aspects come to mind. For instance, broad environmental attitudes towards PDM – favourable or unfavourable changes will have significant implications. Examples could be:

1 Out of hours operations – primarily deliveries – will have impact on cost profiles. Vehicle access controls will have similar problems for costs.
2 Vehicle size controls will have a major effect on the entire distribution operation.
3 EEC regulations and harmonisation not only for distribution but also

product design, specification or ingredients are capable of producing major indirect influences.

Changes in this aspect of the PDM system, that is the philosophical or conceptual context of distribution, are clearly difficult to monitor and even harder to predict. They can nevertheless be vital.

C   Current system capability

The previous chapter discussed system cost-effectiveness at some length. The purpose of this part of the distribution audit is to appraise the entire system from a cost effectiveness point of view. In so doing it will consider two basic aspects: costs and throughput.

Cost and throughput levels will be used to derive measures of the basic capacity utilisation performance of the total system and of the individual physical distribution elements comprising the corporate physical distribution structure, i.e. facilities, inventory, transportation, communications and unitisation. In addition system feasibility should be established, in growth situations it is essential to know in throughput terms the maximum levels at which the system can operate and the cost penalties involved when specified levels are exceeded or indeed when minimum levels are not achieved. Service must be included in this review for service is usually the variable which is monitored against cost.

In order to assess system capability, cost and service date must be collected on a regular ongoing basis. The precise items for which cost/service data will be assembled will obviously vary from company to company. Some of the commonly used items are:

Capacity utilisation	– Warehouse
	– Transportation
	– Flexibility and expansion scope
Warehouse facilities	– Total costs
	– Age and maintenance costs
	– Flexibility throughput/period
	– Total throughput/period
	– Returns handled – number
	– recovery time
	– Picking accuracy
	– Service levels/Back orders
	– Cube utilisation
	– Cost of Cube bought out

Inventory	
	– Total inventory holding costs
	– Product group costs
	– Service levels – total
	– plant
	– field
	– Field inventory holding costs
	– Transfers – number
	– volume
	– Stock out effects – loss of business
	– rectification costs

Transportation	
	– Total costs
	– Production to field units
	– Field units to customers
	– Vehicle utilisation
	– Vehicle cube utilisation
	– Total volumes shipped
	– Costs per mile – volumes shipped
	– cases/pallets shipped
	– Costs of services bought out
	– Costs by mode/comparisons

Communications

– Total costs
– Order communication times – method
                        – cost
– Time and costs per line item per order
  method for:

       – order processing and registration
       – credit investigation
       – invoice and delivery note prepara-
        tion
       – statement preparation

– Number and cost of customer queries
– Salesmen's   – calls/day
                – calls/territory/day
                – calls/product group/day
                – calls/customer group/day
– Salesmen's use of time
           – selling
           – inventory checking

	– merchandising
	– order progressing
Unitisation	– Total costs
	– Volumes shipped
	– Unitisation method/proportions of
	– pallets
	– roll pallets
	– containers
	– Costs of assembly and handling by load type
Service achieved (By market segment)	– Total costs
	– Service levels operated/costs
	– Delivery times
	– Delivery reliability
	– Order processing and progressing
	– Order picking efficiency
	– Claims procedure/time/cost
Volume throughput	– Total throughput – volume
	– weight
	– units
	– Total costs
	– Throughput/field locations – volume
	– weight
	– units
	– Throughput fluctuations
	– Flexibility (capacity availability/time)

3   The competitive audit

Beyond the evaluation of competitors' customers (who represent potential customers) the quality of competitors' distribution service must be established and monitored regularly. In particular it is necessary to know what speed of delivery is provided by major competitors; the consistency of their delivery service and the level of availability offered on a regular basis. The benefits to be obtained are twofold – there is the opportunity that a lack of competitive service may offer and more importantly, there is the reduction of the danger of attempting to design a system to eliminate a non-existent competitive advantage. A complete review of competitive marketing activities facilitates this analysis. This review should consider – market/segment share(s), channels used, pricing and discount policies, promotion policies and product range. Often correlation can be found between competitors distribution service offerings and market/segment share(s).

4   The consumer service audit

A number of consumer objectives were discussed earlier, viz. value for money; convenience; availability and choice. To these should be added location of customers, their current and estimated future demands and purchase volume and frequency. These latter items provide a profile of the nature of the physical demand for our products whilst the former refer more specifically to the benefits that the customer seeks. The extent to which our distribution service offering meets these present and potential requirements of the customer will determine long run profitability.

Value for money, the perceived relationship between price and value (seen maybe as quality but possibly some other feature) must be clearly established and monitored for change.

Convenience, or ease of purchase must be ascertained, together with choice or preference of purchase point or location. There are major guides to channel/outlet selection. Consumer behaviour when faced with an out of stock situation should play a major part in determining availability (or service levels) throughout the channel. Purchase volumes and frequencies are also a major outlet selection influence and as such clearly need constant review.

Finally, the economic viability, not only of specific outlets, availability and product range policies, but of specific product/markets can be determined by analysis of purchasing volumes and frequencies and current and estimated future demand.

Summary

The distribution audit emerges as a key activity in the distribution planning and control cycle. We have seen how, unlike the traditional accounting audit which occurs at regular intervals, the distribution audit should be a continuous monitoring procedure.

It was suggested that there were four major components in the distribution audit: the channel audit; the PDM audit; the competitive audit; and the customer service audit.

The results of each monitoring procedure must somehow be incorporated into management decision making. In other words we have structured an information system with great potential power. How we might release this power is considered in the following chapters.

6 Defining distribution missions

Introduction

It was earlier suggested that a corporate mission is a long term view of what the business is or should become. This basic issue is: 'What is our business – and what should it be?' The purpose of this chapter is to consider how the missions concept can be utilised for physical distribution planning.

We must obviously start with the purpose of the firm and ask the question not only of corporate management but also of its 'stakeholders'. The term 'stakeholder' refers to all those persons and organisations that have an interest in the well being of the firm. Included as stakeholders are employees, suppliers, customers, consumers, bankers and service organisations, as well as the more obvious shareholders.

Each group will have somewhat different objectives. Employees will seek a fair rate of return for their efforts and security of income. Suppliers will seek reliability of payment for goods and services and a long term relationship in which the firm grows and prospers (service organisations could well be included here). Customers will seek value for money in terms of quality and reliability, possibly looking for a range of products, good availability and a return on their investment of time and money. Consumers will also seek value for money, product availability, choice and convenience. Banks and other financial institutions are likely to look for reliability of past earnings and a potential growth pattern for the future within product market fields seen as profitable and relatively free of risk.

Already some suggestions are beginning to emerge which could help with the definition of missions. Product development is one possibility – concentrated effort here could provide the answer to growth requirements and to product range requirements. Distribution outlets themselves can provide the basis for mission definition so too could outlet types in that customers will seek a stable and mutually profitable relationship with suppliers. An extension of such customer considerations suggest customer service as another basis for mission definition.

Whatever the chosen basis for mission definition it must pay regard to the company's distinctive competences. It will be remembered from the early discussion on this topic that distinctive competence relates to the exclusive expertise that a company may have developed in one or more areas of operational management; in other words those things a firm does well, preferably better than its competitors. Some companies are particularly good in marketing, others in production, finance, and other functional areas of the business. Thus a possible means by which missions could be defined is to search for areas within the company's operations for distinctive competence.

How can all this be done? Adler [1] discusses 'marketing vision' as a concept which, once acknowledged and accepted, can develop the corporate vision necessary to take advantage of business opportunities. He develops an idea suggested by McKay [2] who proposed:

> This Vision . . . should be spelled out in terms of (a) customers and markets, (b) products and services, (c) technology and production capability and (d) corporate personality and character – all geared to the satisfaction of customer wants and needs.

The argument is developed to suggest that vision has both width – to ensure continued growth and to dissuade competition by defining the operation broadly enough, and depth – a corporate core which gives the company vitality and enables the company to develop and make greater than average profits.

This approach enables corporate expertise and skills to be identified and developed. These skills can differ markedly; Coca-Cola's strength has been seen as its distribution network – well over 1,600,000 outlets worldwide; Procter and Gamble's strength is its marketing management philosophy whereby careful product – market testing, high product quality, superb merchandising skill and well supported brand managers are combined in a determined and unified manner to bring the company considerable success.

Clearly, the basis for success is enhanced if the 'vision' or, in our terminology the mission, is organised or channelled into manageable dimensions based on McKay's four areas. In an earlier chapter it was suggested that missions be defined in terms of marketing, technology or manufacturing expertise. McKay's areas are similar and could form the basis for corporate missions.

The approach taken by the International Mineral and Chemicals Corporation (see Chapter 3) illustrates this point. Some particular problems faced IMCC's fertiliser business. Their customers, fertiliser companies, had problems forecasting sales on a territory basis. In addition they had sales management problems. These and other problems were uncovered by a detailed nationwide research study. As a result of these findings IMCC established within its own operation, a management consulting organisation which was freely available to its customers. Results justified the steps taken, their customers had been provided with a solid reason for preferring to do business with IMCC rather than any other chemical company in the same field. Sales rose rapidly, raising commodities such as potash out of the commodity class.

Adler summarises this approach extremely well by saying:

> In redefining their businesses in these unique and exciting ways, the most successful concerns have perceived that the core of a business is often a concept, a philosophy, a policy, a talent, an orientation towards a market, a capacity to fill a certain customer need. It is *less often* [italics the authors'] identified with a particular product, a process, a set of procedures, or a supply of raw materials.

Distribution mission definition

The basis for mission definition, as we have seen, starts with an answer to a basic question concerning the current – and the future – purpose of the company. There is an inherent need to relate purpose both vertically and horizontally to enable the company to plan and to co-ordinate its plans.

To do this it is necessary to make some assumptions concerning the overall planning activity within companies. It is first assumed that companies have basic objectives in terms of both economic and non-economic performance. Once established, objectives are published and thus all members of the company are aware of them; implicit in this process is the fact that there are a number of interested parties and that the firm has operating constraints imposed upon it by its internal and external environments. In addition there are internal strengths and weaknesses relating to its competitive position, financial structure and production capabilities.

Defining corporate objectives in this way allows missions to be delineated according to technological or manufacturing capability, or market outlet characteristics. From this it also follows that the conventional functions of production, finance and marketing can define missions and mission goals which align with the product market missions. Hence we get marketing missions, production missions and distribution missions, as Figure 6.1 illustrates.

Goals for functional missions will clearly be interrelated with each other and will reflect the product market mission goals. In the example above the

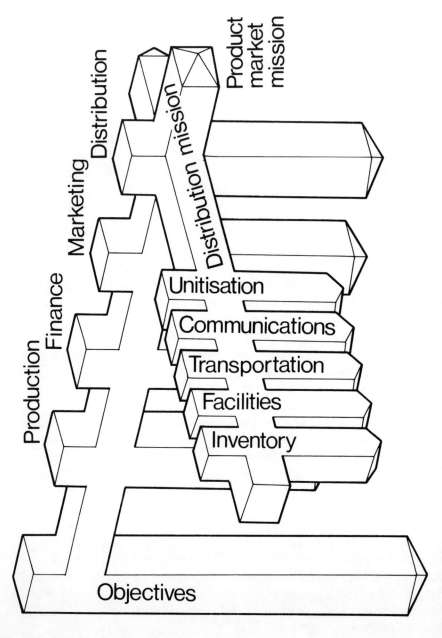

Figure 6.1   Objectives, product market missions, functional missions

marketing mission will indicate specific product throughput through specified outlets. The distribution mission will obviously need to state the distribution function's goals in terms of the outlets to be serviced. This implies that within any one product market mission there is likely to be more than one distribution mission.

Alternative systems concepts are arrived at by examination of the five distribution functions, i.e. facilities locations, transportation capability, inventory allocation, communications networks and unitisation. System capabilities are performance measures of combinations of the functions, designed to meet the mission requirements.

The distribution functions must then be analysed for the most suitable combination of alternative system concepts which will meet these mission requirements at the best cost effectiveness level.

Immediately it can be seen that at the planning stage it is important to define the product market missions and to analyse and forecast their future development. From this stage the product market mission goals and the distribution mission goals must then be determined and in turn the mission requirements as they are now and as they may be over the forecast period. This is very necessary because of the type of decisions regarding investment in distribution facilities that are required.

The system capabilities must be appraised in terms of the evaluation criteria. These will vary. First, they must be based upon the overall objectives of the company, thus one series of criteria will involve such aspects as: capital utilisation, labour utilisation, asset base constraints and other company objectives. Secondly, they must also include flexibility, reliability and maintainability.

However, we have two basic problems remaining. How exactly do we define the distribution missions within the product-market missions? Once done how do we measure the effectiveness of the distribution missions?

In Figure 6.2 four possible bases for defining distribution missions are shown, any one of which could prove to be appropriate, depending upon circumstance.

1 Product type

Product type can be an appropriate base for mission definition because it can enable the company to align production and marketing efforts with products. In Figure 6.2 we have shown four characteristics, which may prove to be sufficiently strong for the company to consider product type as a dimension for mission definition.

The first consideration is life span. This could refer to shelf life in terms

67

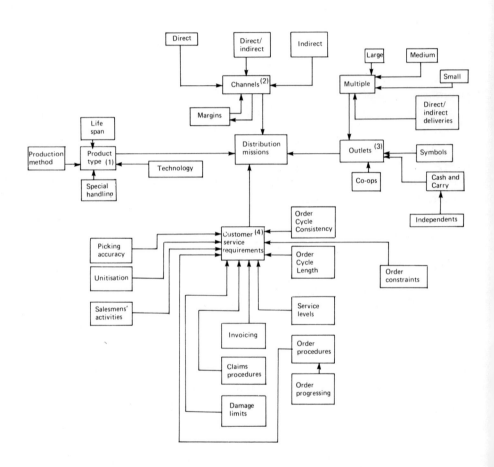

Figure 6.2   Defining distribution missions

of perishability or it could refer to the life cycle aspect of a fashion type good. For both product types rapid delivery into a large number of outlets is necessary.

For perishable products (foodstuffs, newspapers) margins are low and therefore large volumes must be sold if worthwhile profits are to be made. Margins on fashion goods (e.g. clothes) are high and so are selling prices; but for a short period only and late arrival in the market place can result in either lost sales or, in the case of clothes, sales at drastically reduced prices.

Technology factors may also warrant special attention. By the very nature of its specification a sophisticated piece of technological equipment may require special delivery treatment, often in controlled circumstances. It is not an uncommon situation for multi-product firms to overlook this requirement and often to find themselves faced with a high damage/sales percentage either because they claim they cannot 'afford' to invest in a more appropriate system or – more usual – have 'never thought too much about basic product differences'.

Production methods may have an influence on mission definition. Certain products may have a number of complementary features from a production point of view that make it logical to consider them under the same mission heading. Thus many chemical companies group their products on the basis of process rather than in terms of markets.

Special handling requirements may also be conceivable mission factors. A recent grocery product industry innovation – the cage pallet – has been accompanied by a number of unique physical distribution considerations. A number of manufacturers have allocated staff and packing lines exclusively to cage pallet orders. Essentially, they have delineated the cage pallet as a form of mission.

2   Channels

As was seen earlier marketing channels can (and do) have significantly different characteristics. The previous chapter on auditing the distribution function discussed some of the fundamental differences.

An indirect channel can have a number of intermediaries each offering benefits and costs and the choice between the indirect and direct channel being resolved by negotiation between supplier and distributor concerning the size of the margin paid to the distributor and the channel tasks undertaken by the intermediary. If the volume of business is sufficiently large then it is conceivable that missions be based upon channel types, viz direct; indirect; and a combination of both.

3   Outlet types

In many product market fields outlet types differ significantly. A good example is the UK grocery business with its structure of multiples, symbol group operators, cash and carry depots, and co-operatives. Each group has a different approach to management philosophy, marketing, supplier/distributor relationship, outlet type and distribution service. Equally, each differs in terms of its importance in revenue terms and for this reason it may prove worthwhile to consider outlet type as the basis for mission definition.

4   Customer service requirements

Customer service is the fourth approach to distribution mission definition. It has much to offer because it does enable a supplier to group customers according to the level of service appropriate to maximise the return from the customer. This approach acknowledges that customers are likely to differ and often this flexibility makes for greater overall profitability. Hence we can group customers according to their researched needs for:

1   Order cycle length.
2   Order cycle consistency.
3   Service levels.
4   Order sizes/unit sizes.
5   Order procedures.
6   Invoicing requirements.
7   Claims procedures.
8   Damage limits.
9   Picking accuracy.
10 Unitisation requirements – pallets and packaging.
11 Sales force services – inventory checking, re-ordering, merchandising.

The list looks formidable but need not necessarily be so. Some of the factors may prove to be insensitive items, i.e. they have little or no effect on customer perceptions of service and therefore are not considered significant by customers when choosing between competing suppliers.

Secondly, it is possible to set upper and lower limits to each item. Two considerations must be taken into account: the levels of service within each category must be set against a predetermined customer service requirement, and the levels of service set must be within budgeted levels as far as the company is concerned.

Summary

Among the many requirements for success in planning is a set of meaningful and inter-related objectives and performance measures. Developing these performance measures is a crucial part of the distribution planning process.

An appropriate basis for devising performance measures might be to set up a system paralleling the distribution missions. The four bases for distribution mission definition suggested earlier lead themselves to such an approach.

Each can be quantified but there would be information problems in terms of availability and accuracy. Moreover for some mission bases, such as product type, the data generated would be very limited in its use.

Equally channels and outlets could present problems because the data showing competitive activities usually takes some time to obtain and clearly is of limited use because of this.

Customer service requirements offer more help because the data is generated internally and such data that is required concerning external (competitive) activities must of necessity be the subject of specific research exercises and as such is controllable in terms of time and detail.

Notes

[1] L. Adler, 'Marketing Vision', in L. Adler (ed), *Plotting Marketing Strategy,* Business Books, 1968.

[2] E. S. McKay, 'The Marketing and Advertising Role in Managing Change', Paper, 54th Meeting Association of National Advertisers, 10-13 November 1963.

7 Distribution strategy: the distribution plan

Introduction

In previous chapters we have dealt with corporate aspects of strategy at considerable length. This chapter looks at distribution strategy in the context of distribution planning. Distribution planning is primarily short or medium term in its nature. It is an operational or functional plan and as such must represent in detail the ways in which the function's objectives are to be achieved. Distribution objectives are developed by the 'distillation' of corporate and marketing objectives. The marketing plan should comprise a series of programmes, each dealing with a particular aspect of the marketing effort. Thus we should see programmes detailing activities in product management, communications, pricing and of course distribution. Furthermore, each programme should be 'linked' with each of the others, thereby enabling trade off potential to be exploited to a maximum and also as a means of communicating the intentions (objectives) and means (strategies) of each activity to each of the other functions – an often neglected aspect of management.

This is not to say that distribution planners should not be aware of the long term aspects of their job. Naturally, depot location and EDP communications planning are both long term in nature but once in operation became constraints within which the system must then be planned to operate. We must, therefore, begin this chapter with consideration of long term strategy and then move towards more operational considerations. The chapter is concluded by an appendix which gives item headlines for a distribution plan and suggested performance audit measures.

Management aspects of strategy

It is generally agreed that the difference between a strategic decision and a tactical decision is that the strategic decision is made during a current time period but its primary effect will be felt during some future periods. Strategic decisions should also be viewed in terms of their effect on the

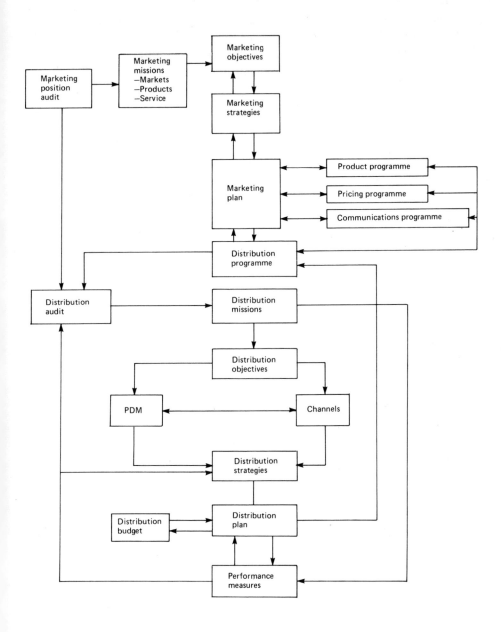

Figure 7.1   Marketing planning and distribution

73

organisational structure, objectives, facilities and finance of the company. Tactical decisions are made within the framework of the strategic decisions, being designed to implement and to modify strategic decisions.

The problem here is of course: within what sort of framework should these decisions be linked? A parallel problem concerns the need to consider those activities of other programme areas (i.e. product, pricing and communications) and their impact on the distribution programme.

Figure 7.1 re-states the linkage between the distribution plan and the marketing plan.

Reconsidering programme budgeting

Earlier the concept of the mission was introduced in the context of business planning generally and in distribution planning specifically. It will be remembered that the basis of the missions approach is to be found in PPBS (the planning – programming – budgeting – system). The fundamental features of PPBS offer the framework against which both strategic and tactical decisions can be made. These have been suggested by Novick [1] as being:

1 *Definition of an organisation's objectives:* reached by consideration of the company's definition of its business(es) and based upon a rigorous position audit. This activity results in the definition of basic product market missions.
2 *Determination of programmes:* including possible alternatives to achieve both corporate objectives and product-market mission objectives.
3 *Development of a planning cycle:* with appropriate subdivisions for consideration of the implications of other programmes and to enable an ordered approach to budget development to be achieved.
4 *Continuous re-examination of programme results:* the consideration of anticipated costs and outcomes to determine the need for changes in stated programmes and objectives as originally established and the results achieved (and their implications) by other programme areas.
5 *Development of analytical methods for measuring costs and benefits:* paying particular attention to the need to consider appropriate bases for cost allocation.
6 *Development of an information system:* to adapt existing accounting and statistical reporting to provide inputs into planning and program-

ming, as well as continuing information on resources used in, and actions taken to implement programmes and of course to measure the outputs against objectives.

Therefore, we can see that programme budgeting begins by identifying and defining objectives and then groups the company's activities into programmes that can be related to these objectives. The emphasis is, therefore, on outputs rather than inputs; on what is produced rather than the input consumed.

Because PPBS cuts across conventional organisational boundaries it is necessary for the planner to identify and understand relationships and inter-dependencies within the firm. This is ideal for our purposes because it ensures that each of the four marketing programmes (i.e. product,

Major features	Activities	Representative documents
1 Define objectives 2 Determine programmes 3 Assign activities to programmes 4 Establish plan-programme-budget cycle	Programme design	Multi-year programme and financial plan
5 Develop cost/effectiveness measurement methods 6 Identify and evaluate strategy alternatives 7 Develop and apply criteria	Analysis	Programme memoranda (inc alternatives) Systems analysis Special studies
8 Use existing reporting system 9 Up-date programmes	Information reporting and control	Accounting and statistical reports Programme change proposals

Figure 7.2 PPBS features and activities (Adapted from H. Koonz and C. O'Donnell, *Management: A Book of Readings,* 3rd ed., McGraw-Hill Inc., 1972.)

pricing, communication and distribution) considers the relative effectiveness of each other when debating strategic and tactical alternatives. For example, an outlet penetration objective may be just as effectively achieved by improving customer physical distribution service (at a lower cost) than by 'pulling the product through' by using an expensive promotional campaign. (The reverse may be true if very high inventory costs are present.)

We have seen, and it is worth recapitulating, that the PPBS approach presents resource costs categorised according to the programme or end product to which they relate. Contrasted with traditional budgets – costs assembled by input type – the restructured budget information focuses upon the competition for resources among programmes and on the effective use of resources within programmes.

Effective use of the PPBS method implies a systems analysis capability with which the resource and cost implications of programme alternatives and their anticipated 'outputs' may be estimated, examined and compared. Systems analysis provides the means of making comparisons between alternative strategies in terms of cost effectiveness criterion.

The PPBS approach does not necessarily require additional information to that which already exists but rather a reappraisal of the existing information system is necessary. Control needs remain the same, i.e. accounting for resource use and performance achievement towards objectives.

Where PPBS is at an advantage is in its ability to allow alternative strategies to be devised and considered. Furthermore, and more important, it enables an objective view to be taken of progress towards achieving corporate goals.

The stages of the PPBS process are summarised in Figure 7.2.

It will be apparent that strategy formulation takes place at a number of levels:

1   Corporate strategy.
2   Marketing strategy (product market strategy).
3   Programme strategy.
4   Mission strategy.

The implications of both corporate and marketing strategy have been discussed at length in earlier chapters. What must be considered at this juncture is distribution programme strategy and distribution mission strategy.

Distribution programme strategy

The distribution programme strategy must be a broad statement. It will deal with the overall considerations of customer service and will contain statements concerning facilities location(s), inventory levels, transportation, communications procedures and unitisation. Within this strategy statement there will be an evaluation or appraisal of the objectives and strategies of the other marketing programmes and an explicit statement concerning how the distribution programme strategy will complement each of the others.

Some hypothetical examples are considered here. A product programme heavily oriented towards new product introduction has obvious ramifications for distribution. The distribution programme strategy will deal with this in broad terms of how it proposes to meet the requirements of calling on an increased number of accounts with differing service requirements and the consequent changes in facilities, transportation, etc. Radical changes in pricing policy reflected in a pricing programme may have a considerable impact on distribution. An overall reduction in price levels (or an increase in margins) may need to be compensated for in lower distribution costs and therefore service. This may be in the form of lower service levels, extended lead times or a relaxation of delivery reliability. The distribution programme strategy will indicate how these problems may be dealt with in terms of cost reductions leaving detailed strategy statements to be made explicitly in the distribution mission strategy statement.

Because of its general approach, programme strategy must be medium to long term in its thinking. Thus it will consider the other programmes in the context of the anticipated changes in capital and operating expenditures with heavier emphasis on capital investment.

Distribution mission strategy

It is at this level that the planner becomes concerned with the detail of the distribution plan. It is now that the relative advantages of the PPBS/Missions approach can be seen. By delineating the missions on a basis which maximises overlap (i.e. product, channels, outlet or service features) for planning purposes a much more realistic approach towards planning and control can be taken.

Assume, for example, that the distribution missions have been defined on a service basis, then because the mission requirements differ (the basis for delineation) the precise effects of changes in mission strategy can be evaluated and if acceptable implemented. We can thus first establish a possible need for, say, a higher service level in one mission than another and can evaluate its impact on mission and corporate contribution.

The result is a distribution mission strategy statement in terms of the use of the distribution hardware items (e.g. facilities, inventory, etc.) and to a limited extent how these may be expanded or contracted. Thus the emphasis is largely placed upon operating expenditures with less detail on investment items.

Again some examples may serve to reinforce this point. To do this we will use the fictitious grocery manufacturer introduced in chapter 3. It will be remembered that four product market missions were developed.

1　A consumer service mission.
2　An institutional service mission.
3　A catering mission.
4　An own label manufacturing mission.

The distribution programme strategy will contain statements pertaining to the overall means of achieving objectives and will deal in broad terms with the interaction and trade off situations arising from the other programme areas. Within the programme the distribution director will define a series of missions that may relate to the product market missions identically, or may differ widely.

One possibility is to consider service as a basis for defining the missions and each mission can then be seen as a 'package' of service related benefits. Contents of such a package would include:

(a)　service level;
(b)　order cycle time;
(c)　order cycle reliability;
(d)　order processing;
(e)　order progressing.

Once quantified these became the mission objectives – the means of meeting those objectives are the distribution strategies.

The linkage between mission objectives and strategies is shown in Figure 7.3. It can be seen that the distribution audit plays a crucial role in the planning sequence. From the audit, distribution missions and objectives are set and strategies developed for each mission. These will cover channels and PDM considerations which will then be evaluated in terms of existing system capability. If the objectives can be met there is little need to continue with further evaluation and the current system

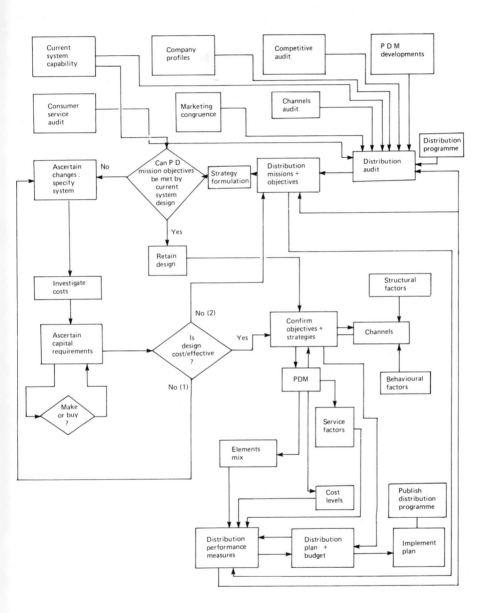

Figure 7.3   The distribution programme – developing distribution strategies, plan and performance measures

design will be retained and the strategies confirmed and work proceeded with in developing the distribution plan and the budget.

However, in the event that the existing system is unable to meet the desired performance levels, changes must be specified and their costs investigated. This will entail proposals for capital expenditure or perhaps leased facilities and/or transportation services. Again PPBS discipline stands us in good stead. Because the procedure requires an examination of alternative resource combinations, each alternative strategy is subject to an appraisal of its cost effectiveness in terms of its ability to meet the objectives set. Again if this is seen to be satisfactory then mission strategies are confirmed and planning implemented.

Should the evaluation prove to be negative then two courses of action are open. The proposed system changes should first be re-examined and re-costed. Secondly, the objectives (and maybe – if doubt exists – the missions) should be reassessed. It may be that they have been set too high and a review of the conclusions of the distribution audit may give alternative views on for example:

(a) mission throughput;
(b) service level requirements;
(c) order lead time performance;
(d) competitor service achievement;
(e) channel power.

Such a review may well result in a series of alternative objectives and as a consequence a revised strategy can be determined. Eventually, a compromise situation will be reached and planning can proceed.

With the plan and budget agreed and published its implementation and incorporation into the distribution programme completes the activity.

Summary

This chapter has developed the concept of distribution strategy based upon using the PPBS/missions concept. It is a reasonable conclusion that in terms of time horizons distribution strategy does not fall easily into a distinctive classification. It has short, medium and long term implications and considerations.

The use of PPBS helps the manager to assess the total impact of his proposed strategies and enables alternatives to be considered in terms of cost effectiveness.

80

The point has been made that planning and control are one and the same activity and if dealt with in this way can make the overall task easier.

Note

[1] I. D. Novick, (ed), *Current Practice in Program Budgeting,* Heinemann, London 1973.

8 Some examples of physical distribution planning and control applications

The central theme of this book has been the need to integrate the planning and control activity of the company more closely with an on-going audit of distribution performance. The models we have suggested are in a sense 'ideal'. Our experience has shown us that whilst such ideal models provide a valuable framework for specific management action, the vicissitudes of the real world severely limit their scope. In particular, the lack of adequate data collection and reporting systems in crucial areas of distribution cost and performance have proved to be major limiting factors for many companies in their attempt to integrate distribution planning.

Nevertheless, given the will it is still possible to make significant progress in this area and an outstanding example of this is described below.

Distribution planning and control: a case history*

Distribution management in United Biscuits

Distribution in United Biscuits Ltd is seen as a vital part of the total marketing mix. United Biscuits differs from many other companies in the British food industry in spending considerably less on 'above the line marketing' and discounts and considerably more on selling and distribution. We believe that we have to be strong and efficient at the point of sale and we also believe that the success of the company's vast sales organisation depends upon a well managed distribution organisation to back it up.

As a result of this philosophy we have invested over the last ten years £5 million in establishing our own distribution system. We have also invested an enormous amount of management effort in getting the distribution strategy properly thought out, the distribution facilities well planned and the day to day operations efficiently managed. Management is applied not

*We are grateful to the Distribution Director of United Biscuits, A. Crawford, for permission to reproduce this case history which first appeared in the *International Journal of Physical Distribution,* Vol. 4, No. 1, 1973.

only to finance, vehicles, buildings and equipment, but also to our human resources upon which the whole organisation depends.

United Biscuits has inherited from the past outstanding brand leaders plus high quality production and salesmanship second to none, but in recent years we have devoted a quite unusual proportion of the Group's total resources to raising the standards of management of the new areas of distribution and management services, by which I mean computers and 'systems'. The results of these efforts are described below.

For whom do we distribute?

United Biscuits Limited is organised into several operating Divisions with a few common Group services of which Distribution is one – others are Personnel, Finance and Management services. The Divisional Managing Directors are free to buy their distribution services from Group Distribution or from any outside organisation, but none of them so far has gone outside. So far all their activities are reasonably compatible and we have managed to cope with the variations in service which each Division requires.

The company's organisational structure is shown in Appendix I.

What do we distribute?

The details of what we have to deliver are shown in Appendix II. From this one will note a total of 73 million units to be delivered in nearly 2 million drops, on behalf of four sales forces selling 500 products in 33 product groups, gathered into the depot system from nine different factories scattered over the UK from Glasgow to London, Liverpool to Teesside, and Halifax to Ashby-de-la-Zouch. Also shown, in Appendix III, is the agreed delivery service.

Peculiarities of UB distribution

Perishability
From this information it can be seen that we have a high volume of relatively small drops to a multitude of outlets. With the perishability of our products ranging from cakes through biscuits to nuts in tins, and stock levels which range from four days in cake to fourteen days in nuts, we have to have an extremely fast moving distribution system to ensure deliveries of fresh goods.

Volume: value ratio
You may also guess that none of these products has a high value per cubic

unit; in fact the value: volume ratio must be amongst the lowest in the food industry. Thus distribution costs per unit of sales tend to be high, which puts great pressure on management to achieve maximum efficiency within the distribution system.

UB's marketing policy
Why does UB adopt a policy of going so far down the trade, resulting in such small drops?

When a firm decides upon its marketing policy it has to look at the peculiarities of the product being sold and the nature of the market place being sold to. Biscuits to be good must always be fresh; thus we have taken the view that they should be distributed as widely and as quickly as possible.

Secondly, when we talk for instance of biscuits, we talk of a highly fragmented market, ranging, as it does, from countlines to cream crackers – a £180 million market going into a huge number of outlets from supermarkets to hairdressers. We recognise that some of the very small outlets are better serviced via a wholesaler, but because of the range and the need for freshness we still deliver orders of more than five cases to as many people as possible.

The above facts have led UB to invest in a large sales force and frequent calling cycle backed by effective delivery.

UB's distribution objective
We must be able to assure the retail trade of fresh stocks, properly rotated and delivered to the point of sale with the minimum of handling, by a distribution service which is wholly committed to getting the products on to the shelves at the right time in the right condition and at the right price. Putting trade through wholesalers or distribution contractors does not usually achieve *all* these objectives *all* the time.

How UB distributes

The depot network
The diagram in Appendix IV shows the network of factories and depots that we use in our distribution system. In total the network handles over 500 different products with no factory producing more than 150 different products. A point to be made here is that depots serve as points for gathering together products made in different factories as well as points for holding stock and delivering orders.

There are twenty Group depots which do all the deliveries of branded foods amounting to 90 per cent of the total volume, spread over only 190 product lines. A further four depots specialise in 'private label' work, 10 per cent of total volume spread over 340 product lines. Two of the Group depots handle the complete range of 530 product lines and several of the remoter Group depots handle a small volume of 'private label' deliveries where the order size is small on a 'non-stock', 'goods with order' basis. Two major warehouses handle the McVitie Cadbury cake range of 100 product lines and despatch to about 50 non-stock depots, some of them located within the Group depots.

Materials handling
In the Group depots we hold about five days' stock of 190 product lines and can organise these in such a way that the majority of the picking operation is carried out direct from pallet to conveyor – merely an arms-length distance apart. This means that our picking rate works out at speeds of up to 1,200 cases per hour and, because all our van loading is done between 6.0 p.m. and 7.0 a.m. by conveyor directly into the delivery van, we have no need to set aside any space for picked stock awaiting loading as most other systems require. This means in turn that our space costs per unit of space are very low. The reverse side of this coin, of course, is that all our loading is carried out on evening and night-shift at higher rates than many other people pay. However, a significant side-benefit of this 24 hour operation is that we can double shift our trunker fleet and hold lower stocks throughout the whole system.

Teamwork between sales and distribution
At the depots we provide an environment for field sales management to work closely with depot management to sort out local problems speedily and satisfactorily. The emphasis on teamwork aimed at satisfying customers' requirements could be provided by distribution contractors, but is unlikely to be so single-minded and effective. Everyone is pointing in the same direction – that is, towards total company profitability. (The efficiencies of our depot and delivery operations are shown in Appendices V and VI.)

The trunking network
The trunking system is an extremely complex one with 1,200 maximum sized loads moving from factories to depots every week, 60 per cent of these on our own trunk vehicles, 25 per cent on freightliners and the remaining 15 per cent on hired vehicles. A considerable proportion of our own vehicles are back-loaded with either finished goods or production

materials inwards; all vehicles are double shifted, 55 per cent of our articulated trailers are maximum sized and the remainder close to the maximum. The intensity of utilisation is very high, with the mileage per vehicle averaging out at 61,500 per annum, or 167 per shift.

Freightliners

We are one of the biggest users of freightliner containers because we find that on most of the longer routes it is the cheapest mode of transport, fast enough for our requirements and reliable enough – except when the service is affected by industrial action. We are fortunate in this area because our traffic flows match the services provided by Freightliner Ltd and our volume of traffic enables us to qualify for favourable rates; these traffic flows plus the location of factories also produce the right evaluation to justify investment in our own service for the collection and delivery of containers. Finally, our peculiar size of pallet, 39 in. × 44 in., enables us to achieve the optimum utilisation of the floor area of containers. (The efficiencies of our trunking operation are shown in Appendix VII.)

Paper-handling – teleprocessing

Another example of advantages to be gained from specialisation comes from the distribution teleprocessing system which gives all Divisions the benefit of extremely rapid post-invoicing, on-line stock control, credit checks at depots to prevent delivery to bad payers, sales analysis, plus control information for both Sales and Distribution management.

The 1,000 salesmen from four sales forces send in their orders direct to the depots, thereby eliminating delays which usually result from a centralised system. The details of each order are fed into the 66 terminals spread over the 29 locations and pumped up the GPO land-lines to the distribution computer in Liverpool where the details are stored on file.

Meanwhile the load planners carry out conventional journey planning; as soon as the planning of each van journey is completed the order numbers are entered into journey batches into the terminals and by mid afternoon the van load analysis of each journey, product by product, is back at the depot ready for use as the picking list. The stock file on the computer is automatically up-dated to take account of these despatches and of the details of bulk-loads received at the depots, together with all other stock movements, such as the receipt of goods returned from customers because of non-delivery, refusals, etc., plus shortages. By midday each day the Depot Manager has a print-out of his theoretical stock which he compares against his morning count of physical stock and he can then investigate discrepancies immediately. The print-out also provides a comprehensive analysis of the back-order file. An example of this is shown in Appendix VIII.

Every month the depots receive a print-out of their revised authorised stock levels for each product which takes account of recent throughput plus any forecast changes arising from marketing activity. An example of this is shown in Appendix IX, and an example of a national stock position and commitment report is shown in Appendix X.

Inventory management

With this sophisticated system how good are we at inventory management? The answer is we are probably no better nor worse than other companies in the accuracy of our sales forecasting and the upsets that occur in production. Distribution makes mistakes as well in ordering stock, in loading vans and in making deliveries. An analysis of recent stock shortages is shown in Appendix XI showing the information that is available to enable management to control the performance of depot staff, salesmen, customers and production. You will note that we are far from perfect. We could certainly improve these efficiencies if we were prepared to carry significantly higher stocks, have greater spare productive capacity to react swiftly to surges in demand, or to minimise promotional activity.

However, the perishable nature of the products, the high cost of holding higher stocks and of carrying spare capacity, plus the competitive environment in which we all operate, militate against a significant reduction in the level of stock shortages now occurring. But at least we know how bad we are and we have the tools in our hands for minimising the problems.

Overall costs

What then are the overall results of UB's distribution operation in cost terms?

Costs as a percentage of sales value broken down into the main sub-functions of physical distribution management are shown in Appendix XII. It will be noted that the costs for which the Distribution Director is held accountable amount to nearly 7 per cent of the sales value, whilst the total PDM costs are almost doubled at nearly 12 per cent.

A point to remember here is the question of discounts; the further down the trade you go for direct selling and distribution, the higher your selling and distribution costs will be and the lower your wholesale discounts will be. It is very difficult to obtain meaningful figures to compare one company with another because of the different marketing policies which exist.

Appendix I
United Biscuits Ltd organisational structure

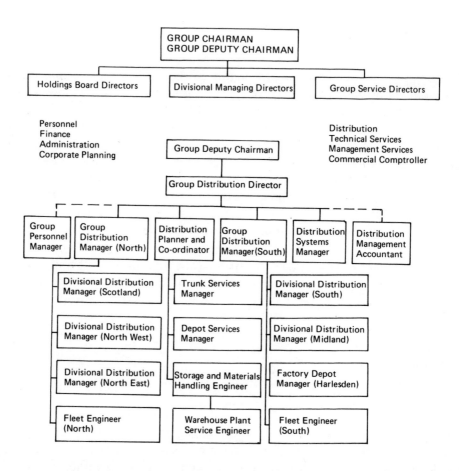

Appendix II
Distribution logistics

Sales force	No. of salesmen	Orders delivered per annum	Cases handled or delivered per annum
Biscuits	700	1,295,150	41,476,130
Snacks	150	249,300	7,175,530
Catering—			
Representatives	70	199,043	4,918,308
Own label	20	115,921	10,669,330
	940	1,859,414	64,239,298
Catering van sales	200	Not applicable	3,930,337
*McVitie Cadbury cakes			
Cake van salesmen	650	,, ,,	4,621,660
	1,790	1,859,414	72,791,295

*Associate company

Factory	Nature of product	No. of product lines	Cases produced per annum
Harlesden	Biscuits	30	13,327,165
	Cakes	35	1,848,664
Osterley	Biscuits	25	4,683,254
	Cakes	65	2,079,747
Liverpool	Biscuits	40	8,418,951
	Cakes	25	647,032
Manchester	Biscuits	35	6,455,665
Glasgow	Biscuits	50	9,189,268
Ashby	Biscuits	144	5,071,821
	Crisps	57	2,692,700
Halifax	Biscuits	127	5,099,089
Teesside	Crisps	53	8,282,612
Rotherham	Nuts	111	4,908,214
			72,704,182

Appendix III
Service criteria

The *agreed delivery cycle* is as follows:

Order frequency	Booked by salesman	Received at depot	Delivered on or before
Weekly orders	Monday	Tuesday	Friday
	Tuesday	Wednesday	Monday, etc.
Fortnightly orders	Monday	Tuesday	2nd Monday
	Tuesday	Wednesday	2nd Tuesday, etc
Monthly orders	Monday	Tuesday	2nd Tuesday
	Tuesday	Wednesday	2nd Wednesday, etc.

This is the worst situation

The *actual pattern of deliveries* is normally as follows:

	Percentage
Orders delivered *one* working day after receipt at depot	40
Orders delivered *two* working days after receipt at depot	30
Orders delivered *three* working days after receipt at depot	15
Orders delivered *four* working days after receipt at depot	10
Orders delivered *five* working days after receipt at depot	4
Orders delivered *six* working days after receipt at depot	1
	100%

On average we hold one and a half days work on hand.

At the moment we believe we have a balance at which point we would make no significant savings by slowing down the speed of service nor gain sales by speeding it up.

Appendix IV
Depot network

Factories	Group Depots
Harlesden	Belfast
	Inverness
	Aberdeen
	Tollcross
Osterley	Broxburn
	Birtley
	Leeds
Ashby	Manchester
	Liverpool
	Nottingham
Halifax ⟶	Gloucester ⟶
	Finedon
	Swansea
Rotherham BULK TRANSFER	Measham FINAL DELIVERY
	Exeter
	Bristol
Liverpool	Camberley
	Swanley
	Colchester
Manchester	Harlesden
	Own Label Depots
Tollcross	Tollcross
	Halifax
Teesside	Ashby
	Gloucester
	Horton
	Glemsford

Appendix V(a)
Depot physical operations, 1971

Cases handled per annum	73,000,000
Total costs of storage and handling activities per annum	£2,600,000
Square footage of warehouse space	750,000
Number of depots and warehouses	28
Number of warehouse staff	770
Number of powered internal transport trucks	150
Number of van loading conveyors	46
Average rate of loading by conveyor—cases per hour	650
Average number of pallets in stock	40,000
Average number of cases in stock	4,000,000

Stock levels of all group products:

	Number of days average demand		
	Peak stocks	Average stocks	Low stocks
At factory warehouses	11.1	7.1	5.4
At depots	5.9	4.9	4.1
Total	17.0	12.0	9.5

Age of stock: 95% of all cases produced are delivered to customers before reaching reportable age:

3 weeks for crisps
4 weeks for biscuits
5 weeks for nuts

Proportion of cases transferred to staff shops because of age: 0.25%
Stock losses: 0.2%
Damages: 0.3%

Appendix V(b)
Depot Paper-work operations, 1971

Orders handled per annum		1,860,000
Average orders on hand		12,000
Number of orders awaiting confirmation of delivery		35,000
Number of locations using teleprocessing		29
Number of teleprocessing terminals		66

	On order	In use
Terminal type—visual display units	IBM 3270	IBM 2740
Computer type	IBM 370/135	IBM 360/40
Computer capacity	144K	128K

The teleprocessing computer has a backing store on disc files of 250 million characters; these are used to store:

    Contents of back order file (35,000)
    Names and addresses of 200,000 customers
    Product file (530 live products)
    Work areas
Rate of activity: 300,000 messages in and out per day
Running costs:
    Computer and terminal hardware

Costs of leasing from IBM plus stationery	£160,000
Line costs—GPO	30,000
	£190,000

Appendix VI
Delivery operations

	1971
Cases delivered per annum	64,000,000
Orders delivered per annum	1,860,000
Average cases per order	34
81% of all orders are for less than 40 cases	
95% of all orders are for less than 100 cases	
Cases per van day	750
Orders per van day	22
Mileage per van day	92
Average hours paid per day	9.4
Number of product lines on Group delivery vans	150
Cases returned undelivered	2.6%
Cases short delivered	2.0%
Total own vans at depots	423
Vehicle utilisation on the road	83.1%
Repairs and maintenance	8.5%
Spare	8.4%
Proportion of delivery costs incurred on hiring	17.5%
Delivery cost per case in pence	2.6

Appendix VII
Trunking operations, 1971

Total number of bulk movements per annum: 60,000

Of this total:	Own vehicles	63%
	Freightliner	25%
	Hired vehicles	12%
		100%

Total cost of trunking: £1,373,000

Of this total:	Own vehicles	51%
	Freightliner	26%
	Hired vehicles	23%
		100%

80 UB trunkers are plated in excess of 24 tons GVW; mostly 32 tons GVW

55% of trailers are 40 feet in length carrying 24 pallets
45% of trailers are 33 feet in length carrying 20 pallets

All trunkers are double-shifted

Average mileage (including shunting and freightliner cartage):

per tractor per annum	61,500
per shift worked	170

Number of locations linked by scheduled trunking system

(including 15 suppliers factories)	75

Fleet utilisation (out of 11 shifts per week):

on the road	82%
repairs and maintenance	9%
spare	9%
	100%

Running costs (fuel, tyres and R & M) per mile in pence: 7.4
Utilisation of own vehicle movements fully laden: 85%
Utilisation of drivers' legally permitted hours: 92%

Appendix VIII(a)
Orders still awaiting confirmation of delivery depot 080
(Date 03/10/72)

Van no.	Reg. no.	Outlet no.	Serial no.	Total units	Date entered DD	MM	Age at entry	Delivery date PP	W	Date delivered DD	MM	Days since delivery
20	21	1822006 7	60618 3	62	28	09	1	10	4	02	10	1
14	34	2211035 1	47825 8	20	25	09	4			29	09	4

Appendix VIII(b)
Print-out of theoretical stock

Depot	Product	Backlog	B/F stock	From other locations	Returns	Short	Other r/pts	Pre-load	Repack	Other issues	Theoretical stock	Actual stock
080	10,815	21,121	16,063	720	16	2	—	2,880	—	—	13,921	
080	10,508	2,398	3,646	660	30	—	2	702	1	—	3,635	
080	10,567	687	1,070	168	11	—	—	338	—	—	911	

Appendix IX
Stock holding calculation (Date 09/09/72)

Product code	Previous holding	Factor	Current average day	Period peak day	Cycle time	Lead time	Total time	Calculated level	New factor	Authorised holding
Large depot Harlesden										
Speed of movement:										
Fast 10014	2,538	1.0	939	1,467	1.6	2.0	3.6	3,380	1.3*	4,394
Medium 10161	766	1.0	261	504	1.9	2.0	3.9	1,018	1.0	1,018
Slow 10479	10	1.0	6	50	8.3	2.0	10.3	62	1.0	62
Medium depot Newcastle										
Fast 10014	843	1.0	377	655	1.7	2.0	3.7	1,395	1.0	1,395
Medium 10161	566	1.0	165	291	1.8	2.0	3.8	627	1.0	627
Slow 10217	120	1.0	12	54	4.5	2.0	6.5	78	1.0	78
Small depot Exeter										
Fast 10014	570	1.0	242	345	1.4	2.0	3.4	823	1.3*	1,069
Medium 10161	443	1.0	126	196	1.6	2.0	3.6	454	1.0	454
Slow 10217	106	1.0	1	30	30.0	2.0	32.0	32	1.0	32

*Due to local promotional activity

Appendix X
National stock position and commitment as at period 10, week 3, day 4, 1972

| Location | Despatches | | Availability | | | No. of | Total | Daily |
	Period	Average day	In stock	In transit	Total	days	required	shorts
Belfast	1,333	95	1,638		1,638	17	157	
Inverness	1,434	95	1,398		1,398	14	78	
Aberdeen	2,792	214	1,099	399	1,498	7	64	
Tollcross	6,445	460	12,900		12,900	28	655	2
Broxburn	8,185	629	4,625		4,625	7	1,270	6
Birtley	6,089	434	1,652	399	2,051	4	747	
Leeds	6,912	493	2,523		2,523	5	891	3
Manchester	6,563	468	10,925		10,925	23	589	
Liverpool	7,373	526	6,894		6,894	13	532	2
Nottingham	5,291	377	2,151		2,151	5	694	
Gloucester	3,354	239	1,351		1,351	5	647	
Finedon	6,896	492	2,022		2,022	4	1,078	
Swansea	2,683	191	1,161	133	1,294	6	384	
Measham	4,757	339	1,719		1,719	5	812	1
Exeter	4,311	307	963		963	3	339	9
Bristol	3,940	281	1,721		1,721	6	340	
Camberley	15,022	1,073	5,636		5,636	5	2,512	5
Swanley	10,755	768	5,594		5,594	7	1,731	
Colchester	3,584	256	1,863		1,863	7	306	2
Harlesden	28,363	2,025	34,906		34,906	17	3,398	6
Manchester	2,660	190	399		399	2		
Widnes	5,850	390	0		0	0		
Totals	136,082	9,762	103,141	931	104,072	190	17,224	36

Product Code 10508 Digestive ½ lb. 20 packets

Appendix XI
Cumulative analysis of short deliveries, cancellations and redeliveries by reason (run date 18/07/72) National total of all depots period 7, 1972

		Biscuits	Snacks	Catering
1 Short deliveries and cancellations				
A) By distribution action				
Damaged goods	Orders	331	46	26
	Units	552	69	35
Faulty stock ordering	Orders	40	4	7
	Units	90	24	35
Other distribution errors	Orders	5,931	976	784
	Units	11,433	2,873	2,386
Percentage	Orders	6.08	5.07	5.14
Percentage	Units	0.36	0.50	0.34
B) By sales action				
Incorrect delivery instructions	Orders	58	11	9
	Units	254	74	19
Part order refused by customer	Orders	499	65	48
	Units	4,776	809	430
Order cancelled by customer	Orders	820	244	133
	Units	28,206	6,160	6,108
Sale of withdrawn lines	Orders	2,153	177	126
	Units	4,938	947	550
Percentage	Orders	3.41	2.45	1.98
Percentage	Units	1.13	1.35	1.00
C) By production and others				
Stock not available	Orders	7,920	1,218	970
	Units	19,466	5,646	4,292
Unavoidable stock delays	Orders	644	145	210
	Units	1,718	686	739
Percentage	Orders	8.29	6.77	7.43
Percentage	Units	0.63	1.07	0.71
2 Complete orders returned for redelivery due to:				
A) Distribution	Orders	667	174	135
	Units	16,480	3,473	4,165
B) Sales	Orders	2,281	574	275
	Units	68,857	13,650	5,020
C) Others	Orders	93	37	26
	Units	3,177	2,655	1,503
Percentage	Orders	2.93	3.88	2.74
Percentage	Units	2.64	3.35	1.51
Total orders delivered		99,627	19,177	15,311
Total units delivered		3,190,472	551,964	680,665
Total orders taken		103,488	20,206	15,880
Total units ordered		3,350,445	589,035	705,947

Appendix XII
Total physical distribution costs expressed as a percentage of total sales

	1972 %	
Transport inwards		
Estimated cost of transporting materials to factories		1.00
Transport outwards		
*Palletisation	0.02	
*Factories to depots	1.71	
*Depots to customers	2.09	
	——	3.82
Warehouse and depots		
*Clerical wages	0.16	
*Warehouse labour	1.29	
*Other warehouse costs	1.19	
	——	2.64
Order processing		
Rental of teleprocessing terminals	0.11	
*Operation of teleprocessing terminals	0.07	
Teleprocessing computer	0.03	
Sales accounting including computer	0.68	
	——	0.89
Protective packaging		2.00
Management		
*Management salaries and expenses	0.17	
Stock auditing	0.02	
Stock planning	0.01	
*Training	0.01	
	——	0.21
***Stock losses**		0.26
Interest on capital (at 8%)		
Stocks	0.24	
Buildings, vehicles and plant	0.46	
	——	0.90
TOTAL PHYSICAL DISTRIBUTION COSTS		11.72%
*The Distribution Director is responsible for these costs totalling		6.97%

Appendix XIII
Distribution costs per case

Division	Biscuits	Snacks	Snacks	Catering
Product group	Branded	Nuts	Crisps	Biscuits
Sales value per case	£1.48	£1.30	£1.04	£1.06
Average cases (cubic inches)	1,058	659	2,106	943
Number of days stock	12	14.5	8	12
Average mileage trunked	111	126	143	106
Drop size in cases	34	35	35	22
Costs per case:	n.p.	n.p.	n.p.	n.p.
Factory warehouse	1.80	0.74	1.59	1.44
Trunking	2.03	1.43	4.10	1.71
Depot Handling	0.90	0.90	0.90	0.90
Depot space	1.11	0.69	1.49	0.99
Delivery handling	1.62	1.45	1.45	1.74
Delivery space	1.58	1.07	2.05	1.47
Management and training	0.23	0.16	0.30	0.21
Total distribution costs	9.27	6.44	11.88	8.46
Distribution costs as % of sales value	6.26	4.94	11.37	7.97

Distribution costs per case for some of the main product groups which we distribute are shown in Appendix XIII.

Hopefully this information should serve to show that one can operate a distribution system providing a high level of service at a competitive cost. Many companies argue that one should not invest scarce capital in distribution facilities just as one would not make one's own suit or cut one's own hair. We believe that in our circumstances it does pay us to 'do our own thing'. We can raise capital as cheaply as anyone else can and probably cheaper. We have a single-mindedness of purpose from top to bottom of the organisation, and close teamwork between functions and divisions provides the best service to customers.

In conclusion I would like to re-emphasise that UB has chosen to manufacture products which are best consumed fresh and to sell them in a highly competitive market through retail organisations which are getting progressively stronger as the years go by. In order to survive in this environment we have to be highly efficient in selling and merchandising at the point of sale, and thus we have also to provide an equally efficient physical distribution service to make the whole operation work to achieve a profitable end result.

Monitoring performance

The case history given above illustrates some of the benefits of taking a view of performance that is not limited only to costs. We have laid great emphasis in this book on the crucial importance in the distribution plan of service. Service is the 'output' of the distribution system, costs reflect the inputs. Since the orientation of the approach we have suggested is primarily based upon the development of a missions approach to planning, it is appropriate that we finally consider how the distribution planner can move beyond a limited cost based approach.

Many companies have no clearly defined policy towards customer service; indeed, in many cases, customer service is only narrowly perceived in a technical or after sales sense. The wider view of customer service, advocated here and adopted by a handful of innovative companies, brings together all the points of contact with the customer in terms of delivery frequency and lead-time, back-up inventory, responsiveness to complaints, technical service and a host of other aspects. Obviously creating an integrated and cohesive service involving all these elements is a task requiring careful analysis and planning. Likewise as customer service is clearly a major cost element in any company's marketing effort, it requires a constant evaluation in terms of how well it is meeting the desired objectives set for it and how the actual costs of the programme compare with the planned costs. The monitoring and control function is therefore one of comparison between actual and desired objectives, with the aim of identifying and remedying the causes of any divergence between the two.

Control mechanisms for customer service can be simple or complex, they can either be based upon a regular review with management intervention when key indications suggest that deviations between actual outputs and planned targets are occurring or they can be based upon self regulating mechanisms that operate according to prescribed decision rules.

From the discussion so far it is evident that there are two key elements in the control system. One is the 'monitor' and the other is the 'standard'.

The service monitor

Setting up the service monitor should be a systematic procedure. Heskett et al. [1] suggest a sequence which, slightly modified, would be:

1   Identify all important logistics cost categories along with other inputs of effort which the organisation incurs.
2   Institute systems and procedures for the collection of this cost data.
3   Identify and collect output data.
4   Prepare a set of desired measures by which the logistics activities within the organisation might be evaluated.
5   Set up a mechanism for the regular presentation of status reports.

This procedure begins with the recognition that customer service costs, wherever they occur, should be flushed out and brought together. Typically, traditional accounting systems will not be capable of providing the data in the firm in which it is required. Many customer service costs will be lost in the 'general overheads' of the business, e.g. order processing costs. Designing the procedures for the collection of this data is therefore no easy task.

Identifying and collecting output data may also be problematic. Output data in the customer service context are concerned with revenue, thus the problem becomes one of pinpointing the extent to which the service package has resulted in the generation of revenue. Obviously this is not possible and so, assuming a relationship between revenue generation and service level, we use the latter as a surrogate measure. Hence measures such as order cycle time, percentage of back-orders, consistency of

103

delivery lead-times and so on have to be used. Fairly simple recording and reporting systems will normally be sufficient to generate the required data. For example, regular samples can be taken of individual customer orders to check on order cycle lead-time, likewise for the percentage of orders met from stock and so on.

Measuring performance within the logistics organisation (the 'process') involves the collection, on the same regular basis, of such data as warehouse costs (handling, storage) and utilisation, transportation costs and utilisation, inventory costs, order processing costs and so on. This data is often conveniently presented in the form of ratios, e.g. cost per case, cost per ton-mile, etc.

In all this data collection activity the key requirement is to ensure that they are collected according to compatible bases. Often data exist relating to these various activity centres but on a non-comparable basis, in some cases information may be available on a quarterly basis relating to sales areas, other information is on a weekly basis relating to customer accounts, still other data relates to factory shipments on a product basis. Bringing all this data together and reconciling it to a common base is generally not possible. In most cases devising an effective logistics service control system requires the redesign of data gathering procedures, as such this can present a major stumbling block. Management objections to such a redesign can be overcome if the payoffs of having an effective control system can be emphasised.

The reporting format of such a monitoring system will vary according to the requirements of the individual company. In terms of the preparing of such reports it is important that the interval between reports should be short enough to enable changes in inputs and systems parameters to be effective. Taking action on information received too late can sometimes lead to a worsening of the situation.

The peculiar dynamics of systems are such that 'leads and lags' in stimulus and response will mean that fine-tuning of the system is rarely possible. While it may not be possible, or indeed necessary to have 'real-time' reporting systems, it is necessary to recognise that information has a value which is inversely related to time – the more out of date it is, the less value it is. One can in fact identify within a given situation the frequency with which information relating to logistics service is required. For example, data on stock-outs, back orders, warehouse replenishments and so on may be appropriate on a daily basis; inventory levels and order intake could be collected on a weekly basis; order-cycle lead-times and consistency on a monthly basis and so on.

At the end of the period – say, quarterly or even annually – an audit statement could be presented. Ballou [2] gives an example of such a periodic customer service control statement. (See Table 8.1).

Table 8.1
Periodic customer service statement

Physical distribution

Transportation of finished goods:		
Freight charges inbound to warehouse	$2,700,000	
Delivery charges outbound from warehouses	3,150,000	
Freight charges on stock returns to plant	300,000	
Extra delivery charges on back orders	450,000	
		$6,600,000
Finished goods inventories:		
Inventories in transit	280,000	
Storage costs at warehouse (1)	1,200,000	
Materials-handling costs at warehouse	1,800,000	
Cost of obsolete stock	310,000	
Storage costs at plant (1)	470,000	
Materials-handling costs at plant	520,000	
		4,580,000
Order-processing costs:		
Processing of customer orders	830,000	
Processing of stock orders	170,000	
Processing of backorders	440,000	
		1,440,000
Administration and overhead – finished goods:		
Proration of unallocated managerial expenses	240,000	
Depreciation of owned storage space	180,000	
Depreciation of materials-handling equipment	100,000	
Depreciation of transportation equipment	50,000	
		570,000
Total distribution costs		$13,190,000

Table 8.1 *cont.*

Physical supply

Transportation of supply goods:		
Freight charges inbound to plant	$1,200,000	
Expedited freight charges	300,000	
		1,500,000
Supply goods inventories:		
Storage costs of raw materials	300,000	
Materials-handling cost on raw materials	270,000	
		570,000
Order processing:		
Processing of supply orders	55,000	
Costs of expedited orders	10,000	
		65,000
Administration and overhead – supply goods:		
Proration of unallocated managerial expenses	50,000	
Depreciation of owned storage space	30,000	
Depreciation of materials-handling equipment	40,000	
Depreciation of transportation equipment	25,000	
Total supply costs		$2,280,000
Total distribution costs		$13,190,000
Total logistics costs		$15,470,000

Customer service

Percentage of warehouse deliveries within one day	92%
Average in-stock percentage (2)	87%
Total order cycle time (3)	
(a) normal processing	7 ± 2 days
(b) back order processing	10 ± 3 days
Backorders	
(a) Total	503
(b) Percentage of total orders	2.5%
Customer returns due to damage, dead stock, order-processing and late deliveries (4)	1.2%
Percentage of available production time shut-down due to supply stockouts	2.3%

Table 8.1 *cont.*

(1)   Includes space, insurance, taxes and capital costs.
(2)   Percentage of individual product items filled directly from warehouse stocks.
(3)   Percentage of gross sales.

Setting service standards

In order that control can be exercised it is obviously necessary that the data resulting from the monitor be compared to some standard of desired performance. This is the case for both the outputs of the system and also for the internal activities of the process itself. Many firms have established cost standards for the basic distribution activities such as transportation and warehousing. Fewer companies however have set standards for service outputs.

The derivation of service standards must obviously be related to the objectives or missions of the logistics system that have previously been identified. In many cases missions are stated in terms of the provision of specific levels of service, in other cases service may be implied but not strictly defined. The service standard is simply the operational means whereby the level is measured.

Examples of such standards could be:

Service element	Service standard
Order cycle lead-time	Nine days from receipt of order to customer taking delivery of complete consignment
	Order transmission: 2 days
	Order processing: 3 days
	Delivery: 4 days
Consistency of lead-time	At least 95 per cent of all deliveries will be made between seven days and eleven days. The remaining 5 per cent to be made between six and twelve days.
Inventory levels	Using an ABC classification system inventory levels will be set to achieve: A items: 95 per cent of all orders to be met from stock

Inventory levels *cont.*	B items: 85 per cent of all orders to be met from stock
	C items: 80 per cent of all items to be met from stock
Accuracy in order-filling	Orders to be filled with 99.5 per cent accuracy
Damage in transit	Damage in transit not to exceed 0.5 per cent of order value

In addition standards could be set for specific customer accounts or groups individual products and so on.

These service standards would complement the cost standards which have been derived by the traditional costing procedures. Cost standards by themselves are of little value as they relate only to the way in which inputs are utilised rather than the way in which outputs are generated. The two taken together, however, enable the missions framework identified in earlier chapters to be made operational, relying as it does on an understanding of how the customer service outputs are related to the various logistics inputs.

The control of customer service is made complete by the comparison of the data revealed by the monitor with the prescribed cost and service standards. Any variation between actual and standard will need to be accounted for and if necessary acted upon.

Summary

We started this book with an account of the systems approach to distribution planning and described the cyclical nature of the planning process. Information, and the efficient use of information, is at the heart of an effective planning process. The intended message of the foregoing material is that the productivity of the information which exists within a system can be enhanced by the use of the systematic framework that we have termed the distribution audit. In many cases it is not even necessary for additional information to be generated – the information is already there but its meaning is never released. Through the effective use of information the crucial link between planning and control can be firmly forged. The final chapter of this book provides management with a practical approach to implementing a distribution audit within their own operation.

Notes

[1] J. L. Heskett, N. A. Glaskowsky and K. M. Ivie, *Business Logistics*, Ronald Press, 1973.

[2] R. Ballou, *Business Logistics Management,* Prentice-Hall, 1973.

9 The distribution audit: a practical framework

As we have seen, the distribution audit is a fundamental feature of the overall distribution planning and control process, and provides data which become a sound basis for all on-going corporate planning activity. Essentially, the audit device is a disciplined approach to monitoring the environment (internal and external) in which the company is operating, and provides an answer to the question: where are we now?

Because of this monitoring role, the audit must necessarily be applied on a more continuous basis than the traditional financial accounting audit which is generally used only at annual intervals.

As a necessary first stage, this particular auditing framework concentrates on six important internal operational factors, aiming to provide information which will materially assist management in deciding how the distribution function within the company should best be organised in future; as presented it is effectively a review of the current systems capability with emphasis on cost and throughput characteristics. The audit can however, be easily extended to the external environment at a later stage, if so desired.

Because the audit is in essence a monitoring device, there is a requirement to obtain information at regular time intervals in order to conduct a comparative analysis, hence, it is suggested that the company should initially audit the performance of its distribution function for three months, at regular monthly intervals; this scheme will then provide enough data to allow management to analyse the results, discern trends, and make recommendations for changes as and where thought necessary. At a later stage the audit interval can perhaps be extended to three months, i.e. four times per year, but this is really a matter of management preference and convenience. It should be noted that throughout, this audit refers to the storage and movement of finished goods only.

Problem

There is one very practical problem which must be faced and overcome in the initial stages of introducing an audit programme: to structure the

110

company's information gathering systems in order to generate the data specifically required by the audit. Usually, it is possible to adapt at least part of existing management information systems to do this, but on occasions it is necessary to design the system from scratch. The structure of an existing information system will dictate what has to be done in this regard. To assist in this process, sample worksheets listing base data requirements have been designed and are included towards the end of this chapter.

Ratios

The key ratio chosen for this particular audit programme is that of distribution cost as a percentage of net sales revenue. In a company where the distribution function is part of the Marketing Department, this ratio would be the direct accountability of the Marketing Manager or Director, and he would be monitored by the Managing Director regarding performance. In a company with a separate distribution function, the Distribution Manager or Director would be similarly accountable to the Managing Director for performance.

Monitoring by ratio: the three levels of control

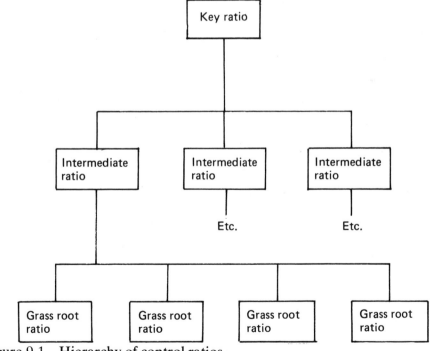

Figure 9.1   Hierarchy of control ratios

Subsidiary to the chosen key ratio are several intermediate ratios which together contribute to the key ratio. In choosing intermediate ratios, there are several principles which must be borne in mind:

1   Ratios should be logically interrelated.
2   'Pseudo' ratios should be avoided, i.e. avoid use of ratios which have mathematical meaning but do not measure any underlying business reality.
3   A manager must not be given ratios which cannot lead to action by him individually, or jointly with colleagues.
4   A ratio must measure a material factor of business, not a trivial one.
5   The ratio of the cost of obtaining information to the likely benefit to management of having it, must always be borne in mind.
6   The number of ratios provided to any one manager must be kept to a minimum.

In the third level of the hierarchy of control ratios there are grass root or supporting ratios which together define a particular intermediate or subsidiary ratio. See Figure 9.1 for a diagrammatic representation of the hierarchy of control ratios described in this section.

Standards of comparison

No single item of information or ratio of items is meaningful in isolation – everything must be compared with a standard to determine whether or not a satisfactory performance is being achieved. In the first case management who analyse the results of the first three audit periods should attempt to derive relevant (internal) standards. In the longer term, these can be reviewed and refined on the basis of an improved awareness of the company's actual performance, supplemented by information about levels of achievement in outside (competitor) companies (external standards). The distribution audit is then conducted at regular intervals and compared for variances against the set standards. From time to time it may be necessary to amend these standards. The following section is included in order to provide the reader with an appreciation of what is meant by internal and external standards, and the advantages and disadvantages associated with each type.

Internal standards

These standards are derived from the firm's own past performance (if records are available), and are generally the most frequently used. The major advantage with setting internal standards is that products and methods are likely to be at least somewhat similar and hence the data derived from records are more consistent over time. There are, however, many disadvantages, and these should be kept in mind:

1 Standards achieved in the past may have been poor, so comparing current performance with these may lead to complacency where it is not warranted.
2 The level of activity in the economy as a whole, and in any part of it, is continually changing, so an apparent improvement may be the result more of a change in the economy than an increase in the firm's own efficiency. This can lead to unwarranted self-congratulation. The reverse is also possible, leading to unproductive accusation.
3 The state of technology is continually advancing which means that a level of achievement which was perfectly satisfactory in the past may be unacceptable in the present.
4 If standards are in monetary terms, they will be practically worthless now unless the effects of inflation are allowed for by deflating to real terms.

External standards

Comparing performance with that of other firms has a number of advantages:

1 A reasonably wide and representative sample of other firms should make it possible to perceive standards of good performance.
2 It is possible to compare results over similar periods to ensure similar prevailing economic and technological conditions.
3 The difficulties associated with in-house budgets and other subjective elements are largely avoided.

Nevertheless, there are problems and disadvantages:

1 How similar are the other firms to your own is a highly relevant question to ask.
2 Just how can the necessary information be obtained anyway?
3 If you can get the required information, how reliable is it likely to be?

Generally speaking, the firms with which it is worthwhile to seek comparison can be categorised as follows:

(a)   industry competitors;

(b)   potential competitors;

(c)   firms operating in fields which the client company may enter at some future time.

Format

For the key ratio, a single summary table is included which is meant to represent the accumulated costs of all intermediate ratio groups for all company locations, i.e., a corporate overview. (See Table headed Key ratio group.)

For intermediate ratio groups 1–6, the tabulation format provided can be used on a per location basis (as in case of warehouse, inventory, transportation unitisation and customer service) or on a corporate basis (as in case of communications). Where used on an individual location basis, simply sum to obtain the overall corporate picture. (NB Costs stated in £ sterling may also be expressed in index form, with the first year's costs as 100.)

Explanatory notes: audit items/ratios and their implications

These notes give an outline of the rationale for the ratios and control items suggested as part of the integrated distribution audit outlined in the following section.

1.   *Facilities utilisation*

1.1   *Activity levels*
It is essential to know throughput levels on a period by period basis. Such measures enable system capacities to be monitored; efficiency levels to be set and monitored and achievement of a balance between inflows and outflows in the total system and at specified points.

The first check is on documentation. This presents an opportunity to measure both throughput and administration activity. Thus we should know:

1   Goods inwards documents: number per period (G/p).
2   Orders outwards documents: number per period (O/p).

Significant changes may mean:

Upwards: that additional equipment and/or labour may be required

114

(particularly if service is affected by slow response).

Downwards: that if this trend is persistent, some adjustments to cost will be required.

Most documents can be further broken down to line items level (I). An increase in the value suggests that administration is improving in efficiency (a decrease would suggest the reverse).

The aggregate measures $\Sigma GI/p$ and $\Sigma OI/p$ gives an overall indication of changes in documentation volume.

New orders shipped (S/p) and line items shipped $\Sigma SI/p$ are measures of efficiency and,

$$\frac{\Sigma OI/p}{\Sigma SI/p}$$

provides an overall measure of service level for the period.

Physical input measures for receiving and stowing goods are useful performance monitors. Dramatic changes in either input or output ratios (see physical output below) may result in flow problems. For example, if the input ratio(s) are greater than the output ratios it means that either orders are decreasing (and action is required by Sales) or that there are relative efficiency differences in the order preparation areas which could in turn result in diminishing levels of service. Goods returned and the reasons for their return should also be monitored. This overall ratio should be broken down in order that specific reasons may be highlighted and dealt with accordingly.

Physical output ratios are measures of activity performance at three important points of warehouse operation:

(a) order picking;
(b) order packing;
(c) order shipping.

Labour productivity can be deduced by dividing each of the main activity items by either the number of employees (or man-hours) or a standard labour unit of cost.

Hence, productivity ratios for administrative and/or physical activities such as picking, packing or shipping can be derived.

1.2 *Operating costs*

It is essential to monitor the changing levels of costs over a number of periods. By doing so, management can compare not only the costs of operations within the distribution activity but also the absolute costs of specific inputs. The cost items selected should become index bases, e.g.

Fixed costs
(a) Leases, taxes, utilities and other occupancy costs;
(b) equipment;
(c) administration;
(d) supervision;
(e) maintenance.

Variable costs
(a) Labour;
(b) variable occupancy;
(c) leased storage space.

Total costs/productivity of inputs and outputs: to ensure that system cost effectiveness is monitored, each activity should be checked against total operating costs. Hence we have:

$$\frac{\text{Costs}}{\text{Goods in}}$$

$$\frac{\text{Costs}}{\text{Goods out}}$$

Clearly these too can be used as indices.

1.3 Cube utilisation

An important feature of distribution system efficiency is the use of storage capacity. Performance is measured by the level of cube utilisation achieved on a period by period basis.

    If the utilisation factor is persistently high, it suggests that:
       – the system storage capacity is being used efficiently, and
       – if the high values are increasing, expansion may be required
       – density of storage is also an important factor.

    It may also follow that very high utilisation factors may be proving dysfunctional within the system. Because of this possibility it is essential to compare capacity utilisation factors with the Activity and Processing Cost ratios given earlier.

2. Inventory management

2.1 Inventory carrying costs

Inventory is an expensive element within the distribution activity, hence two values which must be watched carefully are the total inventory value and the cost of holding that inventory.

    Stock holding proportions by location should be monitored together with transfers (see 2.4) because together they indicate the effectiveness of stock location decisions.

2.2 Stock turn velocity

This ratio indicates the efficiency of inventory management. If the value is low it increases such costs as:

(a) cost of holding inventory;
(b) insurance;
(c) obsolescence and therefore write-offs and mark-downs;
(d) poor cube utilisation.

Conversely a high value may lead to out-of-stock situations and consequently lower levels of customer service.

It is important that stock turn values be measured in the same units to give a measure of physical movement. If stock at cost is divided into sales at selling, the result will show not the physical stock turn but the turnover of the money invested in stock (an element of current asset turnover). Both values are useful measures.

2.3 Stock shrinkage

Stock losses at each location will provide shrinkage rates and indicate the need for increased attention to security.

2.4 Intra-company transfers

These will be a useful measure of stock allocation/demand decisions. It will also validate assumptions about regional demand differences.

2.5 Service level(s)

These provide an important indication of the availability of inventory to meet customers' orders. High levels of availability are extremely costly and often unnecessary. As a further check this ratio should be cross referred to the total costs of inventory and business done with important customers to ensure that service levels are appropriate.

2.6 Stock rotation

Average age of stock (by product group and by location) will indicate efficiency of stock rotation. A weighted average age of stock calculation should be used. Correct stock rotation procedures are critical in order to keep obsolescent stocks to a minimum. A FIFO* basis should be used to

*First in First out.

ensure that it is sold while in a serviceable condition; two measures can be incorporated:

1 *Average length of stock life;* which should be compared with prescribed shelf life.
2 *Total value of write-offs;* expressed as a percentage of total inventory holding and of sales. The proportional change in write-offs should be compared with the accompanying change in sales. The point behind this latter measure is that increased obsolescence may be necessary (and within acceptable limits) if a larger proportion of sales increase is apparent.

2.7 Stock out performance
This involves three measures as follows:

1 *Stock coverage:* Stock should be sufficient to cover the requirements for the average order cycle time. If it is less, then clearly stock outs are highly probable. Too high implies that inventory levels are excessive and an examination by product group/customer group should be conducted.
2 *Order cycle length and production replenishment cycle length* are the two measures which relate flow of inventory into and out of the stock holding points within the system. Each comprises three components:
   (a) *Order cycle length* – Order transmission
   　　　　　　　　　　　　 – Order assembly (picking and packing)
   　　　　　　　　　　　　 – Transportation (delivery)
   (b) *Production/replenishment* – Factory order transmission
   (c) *Cycle length* 　　　　　　　 – Manufacturing
   　　　　　　　　　　　　 – Delivery to field locations

3. Transportation

3.1 Operating costs
There are some basic indices, and these concern:

1 Investment in vehicles.
2 Depreciation allowances.
3 Fleet maintenance costs.
4 Management and supervisory costs.
5 Variable running costs.
6 Vehicle hire charges.
7 Contract carriers charges.

These factors provide longitudinal measures of transport efficiency in terms of cost per kilometre.

3.2 *Transport task performance*

This monitors the tonnes carried and distances travelled by own-fleet, hire, and contractors' vehicles.

Utilisation can be measured by monitoring the basic performance characteristics of transportation including:

1   Distance.
2   Weight.
3   Capacity.
4   Time.   averages per vehicle
5   Number of drops.   per weight/distance,
6   Drop sizes.   etc.
7   Loading time.
8   Down time.

Other important measures include refused deliveries – an increase in which would require a review of customer service policies and vehicle schedules and vehicle hire charges – an unwarranted increase in costs of hired vehicles should be compared with overall utilisation measures (see above). If there is no major change to be seen in the utilisation factors then additional investment in vehicles may be justifiable.

4. *Communications*

4.1 *Operating costs*

As in the case of transportation, basic cost elements (fixed and variable) have to be summed to obtain a primary measure of operating costs; these should include:

1   Investment in equipment and long leases.
2   Management and supervisory costs.
3   Variable costs such as:
    (a)   staffing;
    (b)   equipment on short leases;
    (c)   stationery supplies.

4.2 *Documentation activity*

This is measured by monitoring activity levels at pre-selected points, e.g. *Credit check/control*. Noticeable changes should be investigated for:

1 Credit levels too low (after inflation effects).
2 Poor customer profiles (sales management problem).
3 Procedural changes may be required (if the customer total has been increasing it is obvious that the number of credit checks required will also increase. Thus we must check for proportional increases in both *and* regularly appraise the capacity of the existing system).

Order entry. Noticeable changes must be subject to similar enquiries. It must be remembered that a decrease in the time used at this juncture may enable low cost methods to be used elsewhere in the order processing activity (this comment is valid for credit check and order processing).

Order processing. It is essential that the total number of orders processed is monitored because this information can be used to ensure an even flow of product and documentation through the system. Clearly, if the rate of order processing is vastly different to credit checking and order entry then back logs will build up in the system.

4.3   *Customer contact*

Activity in this area is effectively a check on the number of customer enquiries concerning order availability and delivery; it enables management to monitor the effectiveness of the overall distribution system. An increase in the number of enquiries will be apparent as sales grow and as with other ratios proportional increases will need to be investigated. However, if the increase is significant, not only does the increase require immediate investigation, it suggests that there is a possibility that salesmen may be using selling time to pursue enquiries rather than actually selling. To make rectification simpler and quicker the enquiries should be established by customer contact point as follows – salesmen; sales order office; field sales office; field warehouse.

In addition the reasons for the enquiry should be logged – order status; expediting; short shipment; documentation, etc. This too, will facilitate a quicker rectification of problem areas.

4.4   *Performance measures*

As a macro measurement of communications efficiency the total number of orders received should be used to express efficiency levels at important points in the process. For example, total completed orders invoiced expressed as a percentage of total orders received gives a broad measure of overall efficiency. Orders back-ordered gives another check on availability. Orders cancelled gives a check on customer tolerance and expectations for availability levels. Credits as a proportion of total orders (broken down into picking errors, damages, etc.) can highlight increases (or decreases) in operational efficiency.

5. *Unitisation*

To a large degree the use of cubic capacity within the system has been covered under one of the previous headings. However, there are a few additional topics.

5.1 *Cost elements*
Costs of materials handling and packaging within the system need to be established. For this to be an effective measure the basic unit module(s) (5.2) in use within the system must be identified.

5.2 *Unit module(s)*
These could be case units, pallets, containers or some other module.

5.3 *Productivity measures*
For each unit type, performance measures should be developed to establish operating data such as:

1 Number of units handled by type and total.
2 Average handling time and cost.
3 Units shipped.
4 Values shipped by unit type.
5 Order assembly cost by unit type.
6 Number of units by type and customer group.
7 Average cost of packing per unit.
8 Proportion of full vehicle loads shipped.

6. *Customer service*

Customer service performance measures have been developed in overall terms in each of the other areas examined so far. However, specific measures for customers or groups of customers will give management a much more comprehensive view of customer service performance.

Customers or customer groups should be defined on product, outlet type, and channel type bases, or more logically by the type of service they require. Specifically sensitive areas of service can then be monitored on a more or less individual basis and should include detailed examination of:

6.1 *Order/delivery responsiveness,* and

6.2 *Delivery consistency*

Both of these measures are essential because poor supplier performance will require distributors to carry unnecessarily high levels of inventory.

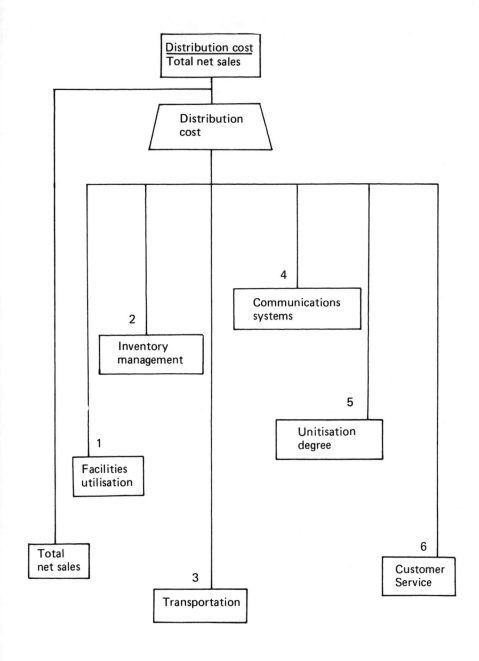

Component elements of (internal) distribution audit

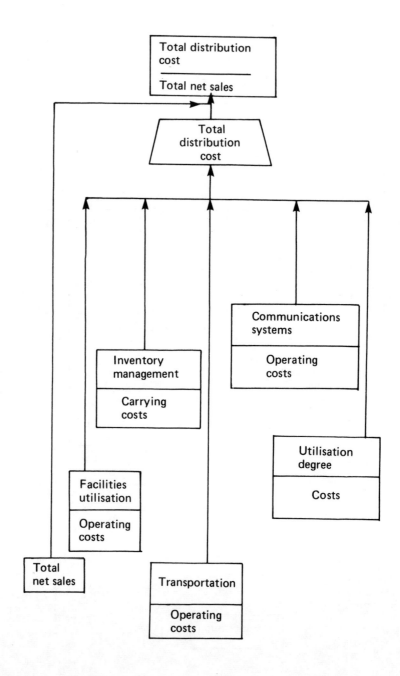

Distribution audit cost trace

Key ratio group

Relationship of distribution cost to (net) sales revenue: Summation of
                                                                 all locations

Code	Item/Ratio	Unit	Achievement record by audit period (p) and year-to-date (YTD)					
			p=	YTD	p=	YTD	p=	YTD
A	Total net sales	£						
B	Distribution cost (B1+B2+B3+B4+B5+B6)	£						
B1	Facilities utilisation	£						
B2	Inventory management	£						
B3	Transportation	£						
B4	Communications systems	£						
B5	Unitisation degree	£						
B6	Customer service	£						
C	Distribution cost as proportion of net sales (B/A x 100)	%						

Note: These tables provide illustrations of the text on pp. 114-22

Summary of intermediate ratio groups

Intermediate ratio group 1

1   *Facilities utilisation*
1.1   Warehouse activity factors
1.2   Operating costs
1.3   Cube utilisation

Intermediate ratio group 2
2   *Inventory management*
2.1   Inventory carrying costs
2.2   Stock turn velocity
2.3   Stock shrinkage
2.4   Intra-company stock transfers
2.5   Service level(s)
2.6   Stock rotation
2.7   Stock out performance

Intermediate ratio group 3
3   *Transportation*
3.1   Operating costs
3.2   Transport task performance
3.3   Vehicle utilisation

Intermediate ratio group 4
4   *Communications systems*
4.1   Operating costs
4.2   Documentation activity
4.3   Customer contact
4.4   Performance measures

Intermediate ratio group 5
5   *Unitisation degree*
5.1   Cost elements
5.2   Unit module
5.3   Productivity measures

Intermediate ratio group 6
6   *Customer service*
6.1   Order/delivery responsiveness
6.2   Delivery consistency

1.1 Warehouse activity factors

Code	Item/Ratio	Unit	Achievement record by audit period (p) and year-to-date (YTD)					
			p	YTD	p	YTD	p	YTD
	Documentation:							
A	Total documents: handled (A1+A2+A3+A4+A5+A6)	No.						
A1	Production receipts	No.						
A2	Returns (all sources and reasons)	No.						
A3	Intra-company transfers (in)	No.						
A4	Intra-company transfers (out)	No.						
A5	Orders processed	No.						
A6	Despatch notes raised	No.						
	Physical input:							
B	Goods receipts (total) (B1+B2+B3)	tonnes						
B1	ex production	tonnes						
B2	Intra-company transfers (in)	tonnes						
B3	Customer returns	tonnes						
3.1	due to: picking inaccuracy	tonnes						
3.2	refusals at delivery point	tonnes						
3.3	damaged	tonnes						
3.4	date expired	tonnes						
3.5	other	tonnes						
C	Goods stowed (total)	tonnes						
	Physical output:							
D	Order assembly (picking and packing)	tonnes						
E	Goods shipments (total) (E1+E2)	tonnes						
E1	Customer orders	tonnes						
E2	Inter-company transfers (out)	tonnes						
	Physical throughput:							
F	Total goods through facility (B+E)	tonnes						
	Labour productivity:							
G	Total documents processed/man-hours	No.						
H	Total goods through/man-hours	No.						

1.2 Operating costs

Code	Item/Ratio	Unit	Achievement record by audit period (p) and year-to-date (YTD)					
	Fixed costs:		p	YTD	p	YTD	p	YTD
A	Total fixed costs (A1+A2+A3+A4+A5+A6+ A7+A8)	£						
A1	Occupancy costs (rates utilities, etc.)	£						
A2	Cost of capital (for building and affixed equipment)	£						
A3	Depreciation allowance	£						
A4	Administration	£						
A5	Supervision (standard man-hours)	£						
A6	Labour (standard man-hours)	£						
A7	General maintenance	£						
A8	Other							
	Variable costs:							
	(volume throughput related)							
B	Total variable costs (B1+B2+B3)	£						
B1	Supervision (overtime man-hours)	£						
B2	Labour (overtime man-hours)	£						
B3	Additional leased storage space	£						
	Total cost:							
C	Total operating cost (A+B)	£						
	Cost productivity:							
D	Cost document processed	£						
E	Cost/tonne goods (inwards)	£						
G	Cost/onne goods (outwards)	£						
H	Cost/tonne goods (total)	£						

1.3 Cube utilisation

Code	Item/Ratio	Unit	Achievement record by audit period (p) and year-to-date (YTD)					
			p	YTD	p	YTD	p	YTD
	Static measure:							
A	Total potential usable cube	m^3						
B	Average actual cube achieved	m^3						
C	Average actual cube utilisation $(\frac{B}{A} \times 100)$	%						
	Dynamic measure:							
D	Total potential throughput	tonnes						
E	Average actual throughput achieved	tonnes						
F	Average actual throughput utilisation $(\frac{E}{D} \times 100)$	%						
	Density performance:							
G	Potential density $(\frac{D}{A})$	$\frac{tonnes}{m^3}$						
H	Average actual density achieved $(\frac{E}{B})$	$\frac{tonnes}{m^3}$						

129

2.1 Inventory carrying costs

Location

Code	Item/Ratio	Unit	Achievement record by audit period (p) and year-to-date (YTD)					
			p	YTD	p	YTD	p	YTD
A	Average value/tonne	£						
B	Average inventory holding	tonnes						
C	Average inventory valuation (AxB)	£						
D	Cost of capital	%						
E	Average cost of inventory holding (CxD)	£						
F	Average inventory holding (all locations)	tonnes						
G	Proportion of inventory held at this location $(B/_F \times 100)$	%						

2.2 Stock turn velocity

Code	Item/Ratio	Unit	Achievement record by audit period (p) and year-to-date (YTD)					
			p	YTD	p	YTD	p	YTD
A	Customer shipments	tonnes						
B	Average inventory holding	tonnes						
C	Stockturn velocity							
	$(^A/_B)$							

131

2.3 Stock shrinkage

Code	Item/Ratio	Unit	Achievement record by audit period (p) and year-to-date (YTD)					
			p	YTD	p	YTD	p	YTD
A	Expected stock holding at end of period	tonnes						
B	Actual stock holding (from physical stock-take)	tonnes						
C	Stock shrinkage (A-B)	tonnes						
D	Valuation of shrinkage in C above	£						

2.4 Intra-company stock transfers

Code	Item/Ratio	Unit	Achievement record by audit period (p) and year-to-date (YTD)					
			p	YTD	p	YTD	p	YTD
A	Shipments in	tonnes						
B	Shipments out	tonnes						
C	Shipments out as a proportion of total (transfers+customer)	%						

2.5 Service level(s)

Code	Item/Ratio	Unit	Achievement record by audit period (p) and year-to-date (YTD)					
			p	YTD	p	YTD	p	YTD
A	Percentage items ordered available from stock within:							
	24 hours	%						
	48 hours	%						
	7 days	%						

134

2.6 Stock rotation

Location

Code	Item/Ratio	Unit	Achievement record by audit period (p) and year-to-date (YTD)					
			p	YTD	p	YTD	p	YTD
A	Weighted average age of stock	days						
B	Stock obsolescence	cases						
C	Average value of obsolescent stock	£						

2.7 Stock out performance

Code	Item/Ratio	Unit	Achievement record by audit period (p) and year-to-date (YTD)					
			p	YTD	p	YTD	p	YTD
	Stock coverage:							
A	Average inventory holding	tonnes						
B	Average customer shipments/day	tonnes						
C	Stock coverage ($^A/_B$)	days						
	Customer order cycle:							
D	Average order transmission time	days						
E	Average order processing time	days						
F	Average delivery time	days						
G	Average customer order cycle time (D+E+F)	days						
	Production replenishment cycle:							
H	Average factory order transmission time	days						
I	Queueing time at production	days						
J	Manufacturing time	days						
K	Ex factory warehouse delivery	days						
L	Average production replenishment time (H+I+J+K)	days						
	If G=L, ideally no field stocks required							
	If G>L, ideally no field stocks required and factory stocks lowered							
	If G<L, stockouts occur unless stock coverage maintained in field warehouses							
	Availability:							
M	Back orders/total orders	No.						
N	Incomplete orders shipped	No.						

3.1 Operating costs

Code	Item/Ratio	Unit	Achievement record by audit period (p) and year-to-date (YTD)					
			p	YTD	p	YTD	p	YTD
	Fixed costs:							
A	Transport administration	£						
B	Depot Costs	£						
C	Vehicle depreciation	£						
D	Licences, insurance etc.	£						
E	Drivers' wages	£						
F	Sub-total (A+B+C+D+E)	£						
	Variable costs:							
G	Fuel and lubricants	£						
H	Vehicle maintenance/ repairs	£						
I	Tyres	£						
J	Other expenses (drivers and sundry)	£						
K	Sub-total (G+H+I+J)	£						
L	Total own-fleet costs (F+K)	£						
M	Total own-fleet kms	kms						
	Contractors costs							
N	Contractors' charges	£						
O	Vehicle hire charges	£						
P	Administration	£						
Q	Sub-total (N+O+P)	£						
R	Total contractors' kms	kms						
S	Total van hire kms	kms						
T	Total operating costs	£						
U	Total distance travelled (M+R+S)	kms						
	Productivity factors:							
V	Cost/km (own-fleet)	£						
X	Cost/km (contractor)	£						
Y	Cost/km (overall)	£						
Z	Cost/km (overall total)	£						

3.2 Transport task performance

Code	Item/Ratio	Unit	Achievement record by audit period (p) and year-to-date (YTD)					
	Gross task performance:		p	YTD	p	YTD	p	YTD
A	Own fleet kms travelled (warehouse to customers)	kms						
B	Own fleet kms travelled (intra-company transfers)	kms						
C	Own fleet total kms travelled (A+B)	kms						
D	Contractors kms travelled	kms						
E	Van-hire kms travelled	kms						
F	Tonne carried (own fleet)	tonnes						
G	Tonnes carried (van-hire)	tonnes						
H	Tonnes carried (contract carrier)	tonnes						
I	Total tonnes carried	tonnes						
J	Fleet tonne-kms performed (warehouse to customers)	t-kms						
K	Fleet tonne-kms performed (intra-company transfers)	t-kms						
L	Total tonne-kms performed (own fleet)	t-kms						
M	Contractors tonne-kms performed	t-kms						
N	Van hire tonne-kms performed	t-kms						
O	Overall total tonne-kms performed (L+M+N)	t-kms						
	Productivity factors:							
P	Cost/tonne-km (own fleet)	£						
Q	Cost/tonne-km (contractor)	£						
R	Cost/tonne-km (van hire)	£						
S	Cost/tonne-km (total overall)	£						

3.3 Vehicle utilisation

Code	Item/Ratio	Unit	Achievement record by audit period (p) and year-to-date (YTD)					
			p	YTD	p	YTD	p	YTD
A	Vehicles in fleet	No.						
B	Total available vehicle hrs. cap. (C+D+E)	Hours						
C	Loading time	Hours						
D	Delivery time (incl. unloading)	Hours						
E	Downtime (service and repairs)	Hours						
F	Fleet utilisation time $(C+D)/_B \times 100$	%						
G	Tonne-kms performed/ vehicle	t-kms						
H	Cube-kms performed/ vehicle	m^3-kms						
I	Average trips/vehicle	No.						
J	Average time/delivery drop/vehicle	Hours						
K	Average no. of drops/trip/ vehicle	No.						
L	Average drop size	tonnes						
M	Refused deliveries	No.						
N	Total deliveries	No.						
O	Proportion of refused deliveries $(^M/_N \times 100)$	%						

4.1 Operating costs

Code	Item/Ratio	Unit	Achievement record by audit period (p) and year-to-date (YTD)					
			p	YTD	p	YTD	p	YTD
	Fixed costs:							
A	Total fixed costs (A1+A2+A3+A4+A5+A6+A7)	£						
A1	Cost of capital employed (at borrowing rate)	£						
A2	Depreciation allowance	£						
A3	Administration	£						
A4	Supervision (standard man-hrs)	£						
A5	Labour (standard man-hrs)	£						
A6	Equipment maintenance	£						
A7	Other	£						
	Variable costs:							
B	Total variable costs (B1+B2+B3+B4)	£						
B1	Supervision (overtime man-hrs)	£						
B2	Labour (overtime man-hrs)	£						
B3	Lease of outside EDP services	£						
B4	Miscellaneous supplies	£						
	Total cost:							
C	Total operating cost (A+B)	£						

4.2 Documentation activity

Code	Item/Ratio	Unit	Achievement record by audit period (p) and year-to-date (YTD)					
	Credit control:		p	YTD	p	YTD	p	YTD
A	Orders checked	No.						
B	Orders refused (for credit reasons)	No.						
	Order entry:							
C	Total orders entered	No.						
D	Value of orders entered	£						
E	Average value of orders entered (D/C)	£						
	Order processing:							
F	Total orders processed to field warehouses	No.						
G	Value of orders processed	£						
H	Average value of orders processed (G/F)	£						
	If C > F, there is a backlog developing in order processing section							
	Invoicing (accountability of Finance Dept.)							
I	Total invoices sent out	No.						
J	Value of invoices	£						
K	Average value of invoices (J/I)	£						

4.3 Customer contact

Code	Item/Ratio	Unit	Achievement record by audit period (p) and year-to-date (YTD)					
			p	YTD	p	YTD	p	YTD
A	Total customer queries (A1+A2+A3+A4+A5+A6+A7)	No.						
A1	Order status queries	No.						
A2	Order expediting	No.						
A3	Short shipment queries	No.						
A4	Incorrect documentation (e.g. invoice etc.)	No.						
A5	Order changes	No.						
A6	Complaints	No.						
A7	Other	No.						

4.4 Performance measures

Code	Item/Ratio	Unit	Achievement record by audit period (p) and year-to-date (YTD)					
			p	YTD	p	YTD	p	YTD
	Customer orders invoiced	No.						
	Customer orders back-ordered	No.						
	Customer orders cancelled	No.						
	Proportion of back-orders cancelled	%						
	Productivity factors:							
	Total number of documents handled	No.						
	Average labour manning	man hrs.						
	Average time/document handled	mins.						
	Average cost/document handled	£						

5.1 Cost elements

Location

Code	Item/Ratio	Unit	Achievement record by audit period (p) and year-to-date (YTD)					
			p	YTD	p	YTD	p	YTD
	Materials handling equipment							
	Fixed:							
A	Cost of capital employed	%						
B	Depreciation	£						
	Variable:							
C	Maintenance and repairs	£						
D	Running costs	£						
E	Total costs involved (A+B+C+D)	£						
	Packaging							
A	Total packaging cost (B+C)	£						
B	— by case	£						
C	— by larger unit module	£						

5.2 Unit module

Code	Item/Ratio	Unit	Achievement record by audit period (p) and year-to-date (YTD)					
			p	YTD	p	YTD	p	YTD
A	Total units shipped (B+C+D)	No.						
B	Cases shipped	No.						
C	Pallets shipped	No.						
D	Other types of multi-pack module shipped	No.						
E	Average cases/pallet	No.						
F	Average cases/other module	No.						
G	Units/customer order	No.						
H	Units/outlet (by type)	No.						
I	Full vehicle loads despatched (cube or weight)	No.						
J	Total vehicles despatched (own fleet + contract and hire)	No.						
K	Full load vehicles as proportion of total	%						

5.3 Productivity measures

Code	Item/Ratio	Unit	Achievement record by audit period (p) and year-to-date (YTD)					
			p	YTD	p	YTD	p	YTD
A	Total units handled (B+C+D)	No.						
B	Cases handled	No.						
C	Pallets handled	No.						
D	Multipack module units handled	No.						
E	Labour manning	m-hrs						
F	Average time/unit handled (E/A)	mins.						
G	Average cost/unit handled	£						
H	Customer shipments value	£						
I	Average value/unit shipped	£						

146

6.1 Order/delivery responsiveness

Location

Code	Item/Ratio	Unit	Achievement record by audit period (p) and year-to-date (YTD)					
			p	YTD	p	YTD	p	YTD
A	Average lead time expected by customers	days						
B	Average order completion time achieved	days						
C	Delivery responsiveness ($B/A \times 100$)	%						
D	Percentage items filled from stock	%						

147

6.2 Delivery consistency

Code	Item/Ratio	Unit	Achievement record by audit period (p) and year-to-date (YTD)					
			p	YTD	p	YTD	p	YTD
A	Customers' orders fulfilled in quoted lead time	%						
B	— by product group	%						
C	— by customer group	%						
D	Fulfilled within:							
	24 hours	%						
	48 hours	%						
	7 days	%						

148

Sample work sheets for base data collection

Each of the grass root items/ratios listed in the previous section has a number of data elements which need to be collected at the operational level i.e. at workshop or office floor levels. To do this efficiently, requisite forms should be designed for everyday use by supervisory staff and supplemented by weekly and monthly summary sheets for reporting purposes, at each location where work relevant to the audit is taking place.

Because companies have varying degrees of sophistication in terms of the type and extent of their current data collection systems and work sheets, it is best to leave the final design of work sheet forms to the personnel working in the client company.

As a guide, the following set of forms has been designed to meet the data requirements for auditing the transportation aspect of a firm's operation. The accompanying flow chart (Figure 9.2) demonstrates how all the attached forms contribute to the monthly report which, in turn, becomes a primary input document for the overall audit process.

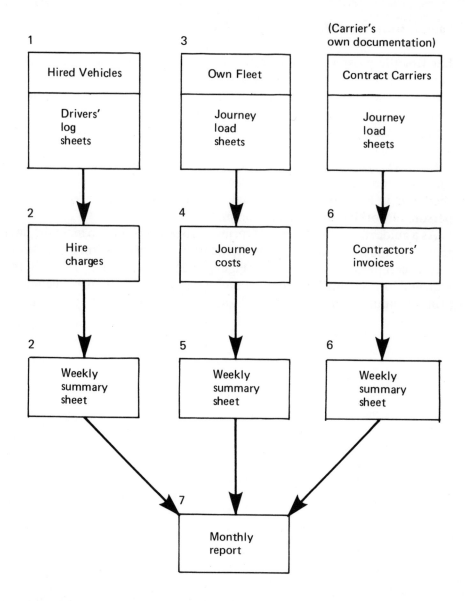

Figure 9.2 Logic flow chart of work sheets necessary for monitoring monthly transportation performance and costs

Van contract hire — Drivers daily log sheet								Form (1)	
Deport location			Van registration no.					Date	
Speedo reading: At start At finish Mileage									
Start time	Dep. time	Despatch load Cases/Pallets (tonnes)	Drop location	Arr. time	Dep. time	Drop size Cases/Pallets (tonnes)		Time return	Down time (hours)

Van contract hire — Weekly return									Form (2)	
Depot location					Week ending					
Vans	Type	Loading time	Despatch load	Distance travelled	Unloading time	Drops	Ave. drop size	Van-days		
Registration No.		Hours	Cases/pallets (tonnes)	kms	Hours	No.	Cases (kgs)	Operational	Down	

Operational van days [   ] X Hire charge/day = £

152

Daily vehicle time sheet — Own fleet										Form (3)	
Depot location			Vehicle registration no.						Date		
Driver		Mate					Vehicle type				
Day	Vehicle hours						Deliveries			Clock hours	
	At warehouse	Travel	Unload	Slack	Maintenance and repair	Total	Drops	Cases (tonnes)	Kms	Driver	Mate
Mon.											
Tues.											
Wed.											
Thurs.											
Fri.											
Sat.											
Total											

Fleet journey costs — Daily and weekly report							Form (4)

| Depot location | | | | Date | | | |
| | | | | Week ending | | | |

Day	Vehicle hours	Depreciation charge £	Fixed admin. costs £	Drivers' wages £	Fuel/lub. and tyres £	Maintenance £	Total running costs £
Mon.							
Tues.							
Wed.							
Thurs.							
Fri.							
Sat.							
Total							

Other charges

(Drivers and sundry)

Fleet total weekly operating costs

		Vehicle hours					Total	Deliveries			Clock hours	

Weekly summary of own vehicle time sheets Form (5)

Depot location

Date

Week ending

Veh. Reg. no.	Type	At warehouse	Travel	Unload	Slack	Maintenance and repair	Total	Drops	Cases (tonnes)	kms	Driver	Mate

155

Weekly summary of contract carriers' deliveries and charges					Form 6	
Depot location				Week ending		
Date	Contractors' name	Journey load cases/pallets (tonnes)	Drops (no.)	Drop wt. cases/pallets (tonnes)	Estimated charges £	Actual invoices £

Volume–weight conversion chart

Because mixed units of volume and weight measurement are used regularly in this audit, it may be useful to prepare a ready reckoner conversion chart by product group classification along the lines depicted in the following example. Such a simple chart could save many hours of calculations when work sheets are being completed on a routine basis.

Volume weight conversion chart (by product group)

Product group classification	Ave. weight (kgs)			Ave. volume (m³)			No.	No.	No.	m³	m³
	Case	Pallet	Other module	Case	Pallet	Other module	No. cases tonne	No. Pallets tonne	No. cases pallet	Ave. volume tonne	Ave. volume pallet
1											
2											
3											
4											
5											
6											
⋮											
n											

Index

Products 67, 78: cash flow 15, 27
Profit: controls 16; margins 21, 26; targets 33
Programme budgeting 74
Projects 44
Promotional expenditure 24, 27

Quade, E. S. 44
Quality control 9

R & D 15
Railroads (USA) 19, 28
Ratios 111
Real-time reporting systems 104
Resources 4: allocation 30
Retailers 18, 26: stockouts 43
Route of exchange 51
Ruggles, R. L. 30
Rumbelow 52

Sainsbury 52
Sales 4, 28, 41: forecasting 64; teamwork 85
Salesmen 86: call cycles 35
Schedule controls 9
Service 41, 60: common factors 42; improved 42, 43; monitor 103; requirements 70; security 55; special 11; standards 107
Smalter, D. J. 30
Standards 112
Stock: life 118; ratio 10; shrinkage 117; turn 117; write-offs 118
Stolle, J. F. 41

Strategy: management 72; market dimension 7; market penetration 22; options 8; product dimension 7; revised 80
Structural factors 51
Structure, competitive 4
SWOT analysis 15, 23
'Synergy' 21, 21n
Systems analysis 38, 44: cost effectiveness 39; elements 38, 44; measures of effectiveness 44, 45
Systems approach: alternative 67; capabilities 58, 67; costs 4; global 2; management 41; methodology 37; subsystems 35, 37

Technological dynamic equilibrium 29
Technology 69
Tesco 52
Tilles, S. 5, 35, 44
Title transfer 51
Trade-off 47: analysis 2; potentials 11
Transit damage 108
Transportation 1, 19, 59, 119: costs 2; refused deliveries 119

Unit: costs 15, 17; load handling 17
United Biscuits Ltd case history 82–102
Unitisation 1, 22, 57, 60, 121

Vehicles, effect 21
Vertical co-ordination 54
Volume: break-even 17; throughput 60

Ward, Peter 29, 30, 32
Warehousing 1, 58: costs 2; effects 21
Wilson, F. W. 8, 9, 10